GETTING FROM HERE TO THERE

Writing and Reading Poetry

GETTING FROM HERE TO THERE

Writing and Reading Poetry

FLORENCE GROSSMAN

BOYNTON/COOK PUBLISHERS

HEINEMANN

PORTSMOUTH, NH

for my students

and

for my husband
and our children
Evan and Ted

Boynton/Cook Publishers
A Division of
Heinemann Educational Books, Inc.
70 Court Street, Portsmouth, NH 03801
Offices and agents throughout the world

Library of Congress Cataloging in Publication Data

Grossman, Florence.
    Getting from here to there.

    Includes indexes.
    Summary: Uses the poems of both established and student poets as a springboard for the student reader's own creative efforts.
    1. Poetics. [1. Poetics. 2. Poetry—Collections] I. Title.
PN1042.G74   808.1   82-4319
ISBN 0-86709-033-2   AACR2

ISBN: 0-86709-033-2

Printed in the United States of America

10 9 8 7 6 5

ACKNOWLEDGMENTS

Ellery Akers. "Letters to Anna, 1846–54." Reprinted by permission of the author.

A. R. Ammons. "Spruce Woods." Reprinted by permission from *The Hudson Review*, Vol. XXXIII, No. 1 (Spring, 1980). Copyright © 1980 by A. R. Ammons.

Jack Anderson. "Girl on a Roof" and "The Party Train" from *City Joys*. Reprinted by permission of the author.

Susan Astor. "Night Rise." Reprinted from *Dame* by permission of The University of Georgia Press. © 1980 by The University of Georgia Press.

Margaret Barringer. "Margins." Originally published in *American Poetry Review*. Reprinted by permission of the author.

Stephen Berg. "Don't Forget." Reprinted by permission of the author.

Robert Bly. "Driving to Town Late to Mail a Letter." Reprinted from *Silence in the Snowy Fields*, © 1962 by Robert Bly. Reprinted with his permission.

Kathy Callaway. "Della's Bus." Reprinted by permission of the author.

Lucille Clifton. "homage to my hair." Reprinted from *Two Headed Woman* by permission of The University of Massachusetts Press. Copyright © 1980 by The University of Massachusetts Press.

Billy Collins. "The Sphere." Reprinted by permission of the author.

George Cuomo. "On the Death of a Student Hopelessly Failing My Course." © by George Cuomo. Reprinted by permission of the author.

Philip Dacey. "Jack, Afterwards." Reprinted from *How I Escaped from the Labyrinth and Other Poems*, Carnegie-Mellon University Press, 1977, and used with their permission.

Susan Strayer Deal. "Daguerreotype." Reprinted by permission of the author.

Stephen Dunn. "Fighting" and "At Every Gas Station There Are Mechanics" from *Looking for the Hole in the Ceiling*. Reprinted by permission of the author.

Jane Flanders. "A Cello as the Other Woman" from the *Quarterly Review of Literature* Poetry Series, Volume XXI, 3–4. Reprinted by permission of the *Quarterly Review of Literature*.

Robert Francis. "Base Stealer." Copyright © 1948 by Robert Francis. Reprinted from *The Orb Weaver* by permission of Wesleyan University Press.

Gary Gildner. "Then." Reprinted from *The Runner* by Gary Gildner by permission of the University of Pittsburgh Press. © 1978 by Gary Gildner.

Laura Gilpin. "Snow," "Spring," and "My Great-grandmother's Wristwatch" from *The Hocus Pocus of the Universe* by Laura Gilpin. Copyright © 1977 by Laura Crafton Gilpin. "The Mittens My Grandmother Made," copyright © 1976 by *Hanging Loose* from *The Hocus Pocus of the Universe* by Laura Gilpin. All reprinted by permission of Doubleday & Company, Inc.

Louise Glück. "Gretel in Darkness" and "Here Are My Black Clothes." Copyright © 1975 by Louise Glück, from *The House on Marshland* (The Ecco Press). Reprinted by permission.

Florence Grossman. "Summer Weekend." Originally published in *Poetry Now*. Reprinted by permission of the author.

John Haines. "Listening in October." Copyright © 1969 by John Haines. Reprinted from *Winter News* by permission of Wesleyan University Press.

Donald Hall. "O Cheese" from *Kicking the Leaves* by Donald Hall. Copyright © 1978 by Donald Hall. Reprinted by permission of Harper & Row, Publishers, Inc.

Daniel Halpern. "The Lady Knife-Thrower" from *Street Fire* by Daniel Halpern. Copyright © 1972, 1973, 1974, 1975 by Daniel Halpern. Originally appeared in *The New Yorker*. Reprinted by permission of Viking Penguin Inc.

Patricia Hampl. "The Car in the Picture." Reprinted from *Woman Before an Aquarium* by Patricia Hampl by permission of the University of Pittsburgh Press. © 1978 by Patricia Hampl.

Robert Hayden. "Those Winter Sundays," reprinted from *Angle of Ascent, New and Selected Poems* by Robert Hayden, with the permission of Liveright Publishing Corporation. Copyright © 1975, 1972, 1970, 1966 by Robert Hayden.

Seamus Heaney. "The Otter" from *Field Work* by Seamus Heaney. Reprinted by permission of Farrar, Straus and Giroux, Inc. Copyright © 1976, 1979 by Seamus Heaney.

PREFACE

It's a commonplace to say that poetry doesn't stand a chance in most classrooms. Whether that's so or not, it doesn't have to be so, and I don't think it will be if teachers will broaden their teaching of poetry to include writing it as well as reading it—to emphasize, in fact, writing it. When we help students get in touch with the poetry in themselves, when we help them discover something they already have—a unique way of looking at the world and the language with which to write about it—they are better able to understand, firsthand, how a poem is an expression of someone else's life and, therefore, they are better able to take pleasure in the poetry of others.

Most young people will stop writing poetry after they have stopped being young, but once having written it, chances are they will not stop reading it. Rather, they will have developed an appreciation of poetry born out of their recognition that we are all, in our own ways, poets.

What we have here, then, is a new option—a book about writing poems as well as an anthology of poetry. It can be used as a sourcebook or a workbook, or both, depending upon the needs and inclinations of students and teachers.

I would like to thank the many friends and teachers who have given me their support and encouragement. In particular, my thanks go to Fran Castan, Carolee Kamin, Arlette Sanders, and L. L. Zeiger for their suggestions, and to Bob Boynton for helping me to get from there to here. My thanks also to the poets who were my teachers, especially Stanley Plumly, and to my students, who were willing to give it a chance.

Stratton Mountain, Vermont
August 1981

CONTENTS

About This Book

Most people have never written poetry, yet most people, at one time or another, have had the vague sense of a poem lurking somewhere, something they had experienced that had to be told in a special way. This book is addressed to you if you have ever wanted to write a poem and did not know the place to begin, or if you have not trusted yourself because you thought you did not know the language of poetry.

This is a different kind of poetry anthology. It's a way to get at your poems by using as a springboard the poems of others. In each chapter, I discuss some of the things I do with students to help them write a poem. Each exercise leads you to a source for your poem, a place to collect your material, a way to trigger your imagination. The sources will always go back to your own experience, real or imagined. Concrete suggestions will help you begin, and poems by other students will show you how they responded to a particular poetry idea. Ideas are contagious. For the most part, none of these students had ever written a poem before. Throughout the chapters there are poems by contemporary poets that touch on the same poetry ideas. The poems of others will take you places that will help you find your own place.

But what about the words, the language of poetry? In order for these exercises to work, you must listen to yourself, to your own everyday language. You must write almost the way you speak, not in the flowery words that are sometimes mistaken for poetry, but in what poets call your own voice. The poet William Stafford says, "Composing in language is done by feel, rather than by rule."

And rhyme? Most beginning writers are boxed in by rhyme because they're busy thinking about the word that will

rhyme instead of allowing words and ideas to bounce off each
other. For now, forget about rhyme. Focus on rhythm. When
you begin to listen to yourself, the poem will find its own
rhythm. It will find its own length. Once you get rolling, the
poem will assume a life of its own. It will tell you what it has
to say.

Ground Rules

- Read the poems in the book aloud.

- Keep reading your poem aloud as you write it.
(Poetry is meant to be heard. This will give you a sense of its
rhythm, a sense of its music, a sense of how the words sound
playing off each other.)

- When you write, let things spill out, even if they seem
wild or unrelated.

- Let each thought catch on to another.

- Go on your hunches.

- For the time being forget about spelling and punctuation.

- Don't cross out. (Later, you can always choose what you
want to keep.)

- Write what you really feel, not what you think you
should feel.

- Stick to the truth
       the truth of *your* perceptions
       the truth of *your* imagination

- Consider what you're doing a kind of exploration. When
you get there, you'll know where you've been.

In the end you will have been able to find a way of
framing what you see or what you feel, a way of saying something you might not otherwise have said, a way, as the poet
Wallace Stevens said, of setting the world in order and getting it
right.

The place to begin is with yourself, with your own experience, your own perception of the world, your own language.
You've been preparing to do this all of your life.

our real poems are already in us
and all we can do is dig.
Jonathan Galassi

1
LISTS

1

Poets are collectors, conscious collectors—of words, of images, of experiences, of a whole range of data. Sometimes they collect in a notebook. Mostly, they collect in their heads. They collect and transform. Sometimes these collections naturally gather themselves into a poem which is very like a list. For instance, if you were to think of a list of things that go away and come back again, what are some of the things that you might include? This is Anne Waldman's list.

THINGS THAT GO AWAY &
COME BACK AGAIN

Thoughts
Airplanes
Boats
Trains
People
Dreams
Animals
Songs
Husbands
Boomerangs
Lightning
The sun, the moon, the stars

Bad weather
The seasons
Soldiers
Good Luck
Health
Depression
Joy
Laundry

Which other things can you think of that Anne Waldman has
left out of her list? Is her list arranged in any particular order?
Which are the tangibles? the intangibles? Why do you suppose
she begins with, "Thoughts"?

The poem *Night Rise* (as compared to sunrise) is also a
kind of inventory. Susan Astor has made a collection from the
places of darkness.

NIGHT RISE

From where it has been night all day
The darkness comes
From storm sewers and wells
From one-eyed caves
From tunnels and the undersides of stones
From chimneys and pots
From drawers and boxes
From sockets, pockets, safes
Out of the coldest cavities of oceans
From the trunks of sunken ships
From the pores of coral
From the mouths of fish
Out of our own dilating pupils
From knotholes, worm holes, root holes
Out of cocoons and pouches
From the hollow cells of bees
From subways, cellars, crevices
From boots inside the closet
From the space between the molecules
From the space between the stars

Darkness, itself, cannot be touched, cannot be handled,
but it comes from tangible places like the boots inside the closet.
Why has Susan Astor ended her poem with "the space between
the molecules / the space between the stars"? If you were to

consider the places where it has been day all night, which are the places that light comes from? Where does curliness come from and dryness? For starters, you might consider one of the following and write a poem that will give us the sources of

grayness	straightness
stiffness	quiet
softness	squeaks
redness	lightness
cold	sighs

Begin by including everything that comes into your mind. Then, when you are satisfied that you have written down most of what you had collected, look over the list. Choose what you think are the most interesting. Try for a mix of tangibles and intangibles. What will help to connect these sources of straightness or curliness are the words that will tell us *where*—words like from, out of, under, in, behind, below. Don't worry about repeating. Notice how many times Susan Astor uses "from" and how it serves the rhythm of her poem. Before you have written your poem, or perhaps after, you might want to read some of these poems by students.

COLDNESS

From a long way away
From up above and down below
    coldness comes
From white and gray ice
From ground
From sitting still alone
From inside long forgotten books
From other people
Out of the night
From somewhere no one really knows

ELIZABETH DICKEY

LONELINESS

Loneliness comes from a lost
Childhood dream
And a boy who never called
Empty walnut shells
And a breeze too cool for summer
From parents who couldn't understand
And a grandmother who died.

LIZA SCHOENFEIN

STONE

From a stone
      comes a color
From a people
From a place
From a time
      and a mind—
If turquoise rides the mountains
Then it also is the river
The stone of the Indians' eyes.

ALEX WEINSTEIN

2

Gary Snyder's poem is another kind of list. If you have
never been around a ranger station or a lookout in the forest
before, you'll have a good idea, after you read the poem, of
some of the activities that might go on there—and more.

THINGS TO DO AROUND A LOOKOUT

Wrap up in a blanket in cold weather and just read
Practice writing Chinese characters with a brush
Paint pictures of the mountains
Put out salt for deer
Bake coffee cake and biscuits in the iron oven
Hours off hunting twisty firewood, picking it all
    back up and chopping
Rice out for the ptarmigan and the conies
Mark well sunrise and sunset—drink lapsang soochong
Rolling smokes

The Flower book and the Bird book and the Star book
Old Reader's Digests left behind
Bullshitting on the radio with a distant pinnacle, like
  you, hid in clouds
Drawing little sexy sketches of bare girls
Reading maps, checking on the weather, airing out
  musty Forest Service sleeping bags and blankets
Oil the saws, sharpen axes
Learn the names of all the peaks you see and which is
  highest
Learn by heart the drainages between
Go find a shallow pool of snowmelt on a good day,
  bathe in the lukewarm water
Take off in foggy weather and go climbing all alone
The Rock book—strata, dip, and strike
Get ready for the snow, get ready
To go down

You're able to touch the poet as a person by the kinds of things
he tells you he does around the lookout, by the ways he passes
the time. Is he lonely? Why is he the right man for the job?
You're able to hear the voice of a real person by the language he
uses.

What are the things that you do while you're waiting for
a train or waiting for the phone to ring? Using the technique of a
list, you might try one of the following:

Things That Make Me Scratch My Head in Disbelief
Secrets I Have Never Told
Things That Make Me Feel Ten Feet Tall
Things to Do While Trying to Fall Asleep
Things I Leave Behind
Things I Should Have Done
Things That Make Me Glad I'm an Only Child, an
  Older Brother, etc.
Things I Would Rather Forget
Things in My Top Drawer I Will Never Throw Away
Things That Happen Once in a Lifetime

These are some of the "things" that students are involved with.

THINGS I WISH I COULD REMEMBER

What was her name?
Where were we supposed to meet?
When was his birthday?
Did I already buy a card?
Where did she say she was going?
What day is this?
What was I going to say?

ELISA WALLMAN

THINGS I LOSE

paper clips
barrettes
my nerve
old relatives
touch
memories
pets
my appetite
weight
confidence
headaches
life. . .

JESSICA NAROWLANSKY

THINGS TO SAY TO GET OUT OF
WALKING THE DOG

— Aw Ma, do I have to?
— I don't feel well.
— He doesn't have to go out, I'm sure.
— I'm already undressed.
— I have too much homework.
— Ask Leslie to do it.
— I'm sleeping.
— It's pouring rain outside.
— I can't find his leash.
— Walk the dog? What dog?

SHELLY MATSIL

In the way that Gary Snyder begins most of his sentences with
a verb, since his is a poem of "doing," Elisa Wallman has chosen
to shape her poem in the form of questions. How has Shelly

Matsil shaped hers? Once you've settled on your "thing," write quickly whatever comes into your head. Only when you're satisfied that you've written yourself out, should you begin to make selections. What you select will help to make the shape of your poem.

After you've written your poem, you might think of other subjects that would lend themselves to lists—the sounds of a city street, the smells of a Sunday kitchen, the habits of your dog, a family dinner in a restaurant. This is material you have already collected or, if you pay close attention, you can collect now. Keep looking and listening.

3

Among the lists that we carry around with us the way we carry around the names of the months and the days of the week are the colors—those of this world and those of our imagination. We could think, off the tops of our heads, of twenty-five things that are red, like lifesavers or crayons, or the way we feel when we are angry or embarrassed. We could make a list of things that *sound* red, like a scream or a fire engine. But suppose red had a voice. What would it say?

    — I'm first in line
    — Those are my firecrackers

It would say very different things from gray or white, who might say

    — I'm all washed up
    — Please lower your voice

In each of the following poems, the student chose a color and gave it a voice by imagining the personality of that color. The poem is a kind of list of what that color might say. Notice, how in *Gray* the list has become a series of related thoughts.

WHAT THE PURPLE HAD TO SAY

I roll and toss
        mix and turn
combine then separate again.
In the middle of the night
I spring out.
I am joined with darkness
        liberated
        when mixed
with the rays of the moon.

ANDREA LABOV

WHAT THE GREEN HAD TO SAY

I am the impurity in the impure
I am thickly built
I am the forest at night
        when the owls come out
I am the caves underground
        when lit by a candle
I am the hawk
I am the ocean before a storm
I am the eyes of the black cat
I am the cream gone sour

RACHEL MILLER

WHAT THE GRAY HAD TO SAY

Solitude
inside of me
You are trying to draw me out of my shell
I don't want to go
It's scary out there
I am involved in my own orbit
Don't ask me to travel
across the universe
to write something down
for you
I am spinning out my tales

NINA SHULMAN

Imagine you are a color. How do you feel as that color?

Does red, for instance, always have a good time?
Does blue sulk?

Where would purple rather be?
Who are gray's friends? Does gray wish it were another
   color?
What does green do in its spare time?
What does yellow do on rainy days?
What does it eat for brunch?

Think about the personality of the color you've chosen. Write down the things it might say—aloud or to itself. You might use the title, *What the . . . . . Had to Say*. Try to let the content, the feeling behind what you're writing, dictate the length of the line.

4

Another kind of poem that is similar to a list poem is a poem of instruction, a "how to" poem. The instructions might be given in the order in which they are to be carried out or they might be presented as a series of do's and don't's. This is the way Stephen Dunn develops his poem.

FIGHTING

Before a battle do not eat hedgehog.
That animal curls up into a ball
when it is alarmed.
And do not make soup
from the bones of an ox.
It is weak in the knees
and you'll be unable to run.
It is good, though, to keep the hair
of a red bull in your pocket
and the sharp bones of a fish
near the weapons you'll carry.
Try to make yourself believe
as the knife dries
the wound heals.

This is a special "how to" poem in that it deals with the ingredients of magic. In the way a voodoo doll might be made to stand for a real person, and pins stuck into it to be like knives, Stephen Dunn makes comparisons. He uses the fish bones to make the weapons sharp and the hair of a red bull to give the fighter strength. He compares things which you would not ordinarily think of as similar but which have one particular thing in common. If the bones of the fish are for the sharpness of the weapon and the hair of the red bull is for strength, which things have the quality of weakness and are to be avoided by the fighter?

The following poems by students are instructions in magic.

GROWTH SPURT

To make yourself taller
you must be prepared
to steal a hair
from a tall
man and a tall
woman.
You must tie these around
your ankles
the woman's on the left
the man's on the
other.
To make yourself grow
you must water
your shoes.
Wear tall people's clothes
that you can grow in to.
Never wear things
that fit snugly
or are small.
They stunt the magical power
for height.

KATHRYN GEISMAR

TO BECOME TALL

Steal a pea from the jolly green giant
Borrow a star
Grab a hair from King Kong
Find a stack of high hopes
A basketball
A set of upper case letters
And an arm to reach for the sky

DANNY STECKEL

TO MAKE THE SUN RISE

Switch on the power.
Let it warm up.
Do not add too many volts
or it will explode.
You must be patient with it.
You must crank it precisely.
Too slow and you'll set fire
    to the world.
Too fast and you'll leave us
    in the dark.

WARREN COHEN

Using the power of the poet, which is not unlike the power of the magician, you are about to tell us how to cast a spell. First, write down all of your instructions, even silly ones. Don't be afraid to make wild comparisons. For instance, if you're writing about snow, which things have whiteness, or cold, or perfect symmetry? Then choose the instruction you think will be most effective in bringing about the magic. The following are possible titles:

How to Make It Snow
How to Make the Rain Go Away
How to Make Someone You Love, Love You
How to Make the Phone Ring
How to Make Your Eyes Blue
How to Make a Bully Have a Bellyache

Here are some more poems for your pleasure. Each in its own way incorporates a list.

MOON FISHING

When the moon was full they came to the water,
some with pitchforks, some with rakes
some with sieves and ladles
and one with a silver cup.

And they fished till a traveler passed them and said,
"Fools,
to catch the moon you must let your women
spread their hair on the water—
even the wily moon will leap to that bobbing
net of shimmering threads,
gasp and flop till its silver scales
lie back and still at your feet."

And they fished with the hair of their women
till a traveler passed them and said,
"Fools,
do you think the moon is caught lightly,
with glitter and silk threads?
You must cut out your hearts and bait your hooks
with those dark animals:
and what matter you lost your hearts to reel in your
    dreams?"

And they fished with their tight, hot hearts
till a traveler passed them and said,
"Fools,
what good is the moon to a heartless man?
Put back your hearts and get on your knees
and drink as you never have,
until your throats are coated with silver
and your voices ring like bells."

And they fished with their lips and tongues
until the water was gone
and the moon had slipped away
in the soft, bottomless mud.

LISEL MUELLER

"Sounds have been dropping out of our language
for centuries . . . for example, the *l* in such words
as could, would, and should has been silent for
hundreds of years . . ." Shaw & Dodge, *The
Shorter Handbook of College Composition.*

SILENT LETTERS

There is little enough we know of them.
They are ghosts of themselves,
wrapped in echoes which will not resound.

Although we could talk of the ones
filled with vehement anger—
the swords half searching for blood,
the knives which light at the
edge of a sharp silence
the combs gnashing their teeth
in dumb fury—
they are most often numb, acquiescent,
becalmed by their uselessness,
doubting they will find their tongues.

The old mortgage lies dead
in the empty drawer,
the faded receipts have given
out with not even a sigh.
The deserted depot listens for the
sound of its last whistle,
and phlegm strangles quietly on a
small piece of itself in a corner.

They look for a sign, for an answer,
they long for the hour of recall.
They soften the outlines of psalms.
They wait at the end of all hymns,
hoping to find their voice
in the hymnals.

L. L. ZEIGER

THE SPHERE

I listen in a small rectangular
room to the story of the bottom line
as told by a tax accountant

yet I know that below the bottom line
are more lines and even further down
are the dreaded bottomless lines
drawn by children with
enormous rulers

and everywhere are the zig-zag lines
followed by thunder and the Greek lines
that never meet let alone drink together
and the squiggly lines of mad crayons

and the dew line which evaporates
as I cross it and the line I wait on
behind other slender lines in top hats

and the faint Mason Dixon and Maginot
and the lines around my eyes,
the price of laughing at the calendar.

So I tell the tax accountant
that his bottom line doesn't make it
to first base, which you must admit is

most cleanly transected by a white line
moving out toward infinity, one arm
of a geometrical embrace in which
men play ball.

BILLY COLLINS

THE AVENUE BEARING THE INITIAL OF CHRIST INTO THE NEW WORLD*

pcheek pcheek pcheek pcheek pcheek
They cry. The motherbirds thieve the air
To appease them. A tug on the East River
Blasts the bass-note of its passage, lifted
From the infra-bass of the sea. A broom
Swishes over the sidewalk like feet through leaves.
Valerio's pushcart Ice Coal Kerosene
Moves clack
            clack
                clack
On a broken wheelrim. Ringing in its chains
The New Star Laundry horse comes down the street
Like a roofleak whucking into a pail.
At the redlight, where a horn blares,
The Golden Harvest Bakery brakes on its gears,
Squeaks, and seethes in place. A propane-
gassed bus makes its way with big, airy sighs.

Across the street a woman throws open
the window.
She sets, terribly softly,
Two potted plants on the windowledge
            tic   tic
And bangs shut her window.

*This is Part 1 of a 14 part poem. Avenue C is on the lower east side in New York City.

A man leaves a doorway tic toc tic toc tic toc tic toc hurrah
    toc splat on Avenue C tic etc and turns the corner.
Banking the same corner
A pigeon coasts 5th Street in shadows,
Looks for altitude, surmounts the rims of buildings,
And turns white.

The babybirds pipe down. It is day.

GALWAY KINNELL

LYING IN A HAMMOCK AT WILLIAM DUFFY'S FARM IN PINE ISLAND, MINNESOTA

Over my head, I see the bronze butterfly,
Asleep on the black trunk
Blowing like a leaf in green shadow.
Down the ravine behind the empty house
The cowbells follow one another
Into the distances of the afternoon.
To my right,
In a field of sunlight between two pines,
The droppings of last year's horses
Blaze up into golden stones.
I lean back, as the evening darkens and comes on.
A chicken hawk floats over, looking for home.
I have wasted my life.

JAMES WRIGHT

YELLOW

Yellow is for regret, the distal, the second hand;
The grasshopper's wing, that yellow, the slur of dust;
Back light, the yellow of loneliness;
The yellow of animals, their yellow eyes;
The holy yellow of death;
Intuitive yellow, the yellow of air;
The double yellow, telling who comes and who goes;
The yellow of yellowhammers, one drop of the devil's blood;
The yellow of what is past;
Yellow of wormwood, yellow of straw;
The yellow of circuits, the yellow beneath the skin;
The yellow of pencils, their black veins;
Amaranth yellow, bright bloom;
The yellow of sulfur, the finger, the road home.

CHARLES WRIGHT

2
THEN

1

The early times and the early places of our lives are a rich source of material for many writers—the sad things, the funny things, the frightening things, the incomprehensible things. Sometimes we are reminded unexpectedly. We might hear a song or someone chanting a jump-rope rhyme or someone on the street bouncing a ball.

A

My name is Alice
I live in Australia
and I sell apples.

It might be something we haven't eaten for years, like gingersnaps, that remind us, or it might just be the way the air smells on a certain day. We can feel the impact of a snowball wrapped in ice.

Let's go back now, more specifically, to that very short time, probably between the ages of seven and eight, when we played the games of imagination—games like house and school, store, doctor, cops and robbers. These are the games in which *we* made up the rules. We determined the episodes and we chose the roles we would play. These are the games in which we tried on life. For some of us, it would be the same game over and over, variations on the same episode. For some of us, it was always the same role. This is the material Judith Hemschemeyer draws upon in her poem,

THE SETTLERS

I was the father
I crouched in deep grass
Behind the back kitchen
Turning the grindstone.
That was my job.

My sister was the mother,
Pounding grass for soup.
My cousins were the children.
They had to keep building,
Trampling the grass
To make more rounded green rooms.

No one could see me
But I worked until sundown
Because only the grass I had ground
Was real food, real medicine,
Real fuel to keep us warm.
In autumn we used maple leaves
In winter, snow.

Go back to that place in *your* life. Think about a game of imagination that you played—boat or army, soap opera or castle, spaceship or jungle, house, school, store, or a game without a name. Once you've settled on a game, consider these questions.

Where did the game take place?
How often did you play?
What was your role?
Was it always the same?
Did you like playing that part?
What were your tasks or activities?
What were the roles of the others?
What are some of the details of the game?
How did you feel about it?
How do you see it from this distance?

The following are recollections by students:

THE WAGON

I was the bus driver.
I would pull from the front.
Uphill — pull
Downhill — ride.

You were the passenger.
You rode on the wagon.
You sat and watched.

No one wanted to be the driver.
It was me
Pulling, ever pulling.

ANDY GELFNER

HUNTING

I was the warrior
I had my bow and arrows.
In front stood my dog, Sambaroo.
He spotted the evening dinner.

My brother was my hunting partner.
Behind he stood like a giant.
Swoosh went the arrows.
Our game fell before us.

No one knew we were Indians,
But that did not matter.
When we got tired we stopped
To let the grass lie still.

GORDON HAMILTON

THEIR GAMES

I used to watch them play their games
Always winning and shouting.
I was too little to play — they said.

I used to watch
Always ducking the imaginary bullets
Living after they were dead
Each a hero in his own way.

Then one day I grew up, and they
Were too old to play.

SETH MATLINS

Look again at Judith Hemschemeyer's poem, *The Settlers*. It's divided into three stanzas because each stanza deals with a different aspect of the same subject, almost the way you would divide a composition into paragraphs.

Stanza 1 — the poet's role in the game
Stanza 2 — the roles of the others
Stanza 3 — how she felt about her role

Notice that the language in the Hemschemeyer poem and in the students' poems is the ordinary language of everyday. The sentences are simple, adding to that sense of a childhood game. It sounds almost as if one were recollecting a dream.

Try a three stanza poem about a game of imagination. To get the feeling of a firsthand experience, begin with, "I." We'll be listening for your voice. In the first stanza, you might tell your role in the game; in the second, describe the roles of the others; in the third, make a connection between what you did then and how you feel now.

2

A variation of this would be to write about a *real* game that you played as a child—hide-and-seek or jacks or blindman's buff. You might begin to think about it by thinking about the seasons. What were the games when you could stay up late in summer—Statues, Ringaleevio, Kick-the-Can, or were you the one who was called in early? What were the games that waited all winter for spring? Were there special marbles that brought you luck? Once you've decided which game you're going to write about, consider these questions.

What time of year was it?
Where did you play?
Who played?
Who was left out?
What props or equipment was involved?

What were the rules?

How did you feel about it?

Who are you now and where do you stand as you
    write this?

You might work with these questions in order, or you
might write a poem about only one of them; for instance, who
was left out. Keep in mind that games have sound and motion.
The word, jump, sounds like a jump. Chant it when you read
Nike Lanning's poem. Notice where the lines end in *Chase*.
They create the feeling of chase and catch, a starting and stopping. All of the following poems by students touch in one way
or another on how they felt about what they did, how they
feel now, perhaps, about what they're doing.

JUMP

Jump Jump Jump Jump
How long will it be
Days, weeks, thoughts
        go by
The chant continues
Too many thoughts
Loaded, Overloaded
The circuits break
The chant stops
It's my turn
To turn the rope.

NIKE LANNING

CHASE

me if you will
but you can't
but I will
        let you
catch me
so I can
        chase you.

DAVID SILVER

3

School days are especially charged with memories. Go back to the earliest classroom you can remember. Picture yourself sitting on one of the small chairs. Who sat next to you? What color were the walls? Who was your best friend? Whom did you fear the most? Do you remember the taste of warm apple juice and crackers? Do you remember the name of the teacher?

Write a poem about one specific incident that you recall. It can be a kind of story, something that happened to you or to one of your friends. Begin halfway through, in the middle of the action, letting each line unfold another step in the story. Notice the use of specific detail in each of the following excerpts or poems by students.

> While serving lunch
> in that cluttered room
> the teacher never looked at
> or even noticed me
> while I tugged at her skirt
> trying to show her
> the first tooth
> I had lost
> in an apple . . .
>
> KAYLA SCHWARTZ

> The day we got our phonics book
> I threw up on mine
> And Karen's
> And Tim's,
> The teacher asked Karen to
> Take me to the nurse.
> She regretted it
> But she did it . . .
>
> CHRIS RYAN

RECESS

The vast savannah
      was our terrain
On which we
      the sprightly gazelles
Fled from the sleek cheetahs
Until our teachers
Whistled us back
      to the fourth grade.

NANCY KOPANS

Write a poem about a particular schoolmate or a teacher.

. . . Second grade
    full of tall Margo
    with the strange glass earrings . . .

NINA SCHULMAN

Write a poem about a task that you had to do in school that you loved or hated.

SCRIPT

We turned the desks sideways.
Mrs. Zimmerman would hand out the paper
with lines two inches thick
a dotted line in between.
With the overhead projector
flashing giant script b's all over the walls
we would try to master
the secret code
of squirls and squiggles connected together.
I was never sure
if you attached the whole sentence
or just the words
butwastooembarrassedtoask.

F was the hardest letter.

FAITH BENTON

4

The exercises in this chapter have touched on very specific places to find remembrances, but the whole world of your childhood offers possibilities for poems. Consider

an early house you lived in
a relationship with a grandparent
    (aunt, uncle, cousin)
a favorite toy broken
a movie you saw six times
your first goldfish, turtle, hamster
your best friend
an old picture book
an early photograph
piano lessons/dancing lessons
running away from home

Begin by writing down everything that's even remotely connected to the subject. Try to put yourself physically in that place. Think of the details as you perceived them through your senses—the smell of the movie house, the voice of the dancing teacher. Write a poem and make your memory so authentic that we will be reminded as if it were something we had experienced.

After you've written your poem, you might want to look at what two students have written—Beth Frost's recollection of her grandmother and Joe Dobrow's recollection of a vacation trip. Each is very much like a story, an incident seemingly quite minor, nevertheless remembered, in which the narrator plays the role of the protagonist. We hear the voice of the child as he or she was then, and we hear the overlay of the voice looking back.

GRANDMOTHER'S VISIT

You walked out of the plane
Into your room
And made it my own
Filled it with yourself—
The scent of powder,
The small leather prayer book
Wrapped in plastic to hold the aging
Skin, worn and wrinkled.

I would wake early
Before the rest were awake
And know you would be reading.
I skirted over the cold wood floors
Held my breath against the stairs' creaks
And saw the light under the door.

I climbed under your warm blankets
And listened.

BETH FROST

VACATION

The smell of fish was everywhere
and seashore
and below the miles and miles of concrete bridge
and tunnel
and bridge
and tunnel
were millions and billions of fish.

The car travelled 50 miles an hour
making two beats every time it passed over a roadway
    seam.
The map of Virginia was in the front
and the back
and between the seats.

I climbed onto my sister's lap
to see if I could see
out the window, over the railing
where a blue ocean was
and millions and billions of fish
but I couldn't.

So I sat back down, stared at
the up-side-down map
and listened to the two beats
and smelled the fish.

JOE DOBROW

Following are more poems that look back.

THEN

In the village the children
were what they had always been—
a girl wanted to be a nurse
or a dancer, a boy wished for a horse
or an elephant up in his bed.
Autumn got chilly, winter hard
and longer than dreams, but dreams
came back, slippery and quick
as minnows. And spring—
spring made you stop, look,
and fall from the sky
for keeps. You had a tadpole
and the whole day. . .
One summer, tasting the salt
on your lips, you promised forever—
and the cricket's song was long and full
before it got slimmer and quit.
But the road and the river
were what they always had been,
and your heart would not break, not ever.

GARY GILDNER

DON'T FORGET

I was always called in early for dinner.
It was dusk usually, half an inning to go,
I'd hear my mother calling me to beat the dark,
everyone would mumble, I'd throw my glove down and
   leave.

At home, sitting at the table, I'd imagine the score,
and the speckled homework book seemed to watch me
until I opened it, stared at the numbers and fell asleep.
Damp laundry rustled in the yards of the houses.

Everyone was punished like this because
our parents worried we'd fall, and missed us,
but we always got hurt anyway, or we'd sit for hours
sanding the wings of a wood fighterplane until they
   shined

like metal. We climbed walls until we slipped and our
    legs broke.
Our first kisses were so murderous we almost fainted.
Don't forget, this is inside us every day.
We want everything, our hands stop too soon,

and who are we when a face whispers and opens to us
like a wave? The tame grasses of the head, the moist
    spiral ear,
some water nobody has crossed—you feel yourself leaving,
you can't lift your hands, you stand there, leaving.

STEPHEN BERG

THE PARTY

I don't care if nobody
under forty can hang a door
properly. I'm six and I'm bored.
In the kitchen Lavada
is plucking a turkey
who looks crumpled
and turned inside out.
He's full of holes.
I throw my skinny arms in the air
as far as my bones will let them go
and giggle. It's ten years to Lavada's heart
attack and sixty to mine.
Black overweight Lavada tucks
a feather in her hair
and we dance, her triceps
wobbling like charred wattles. We laugh
until our jawbones sting
as if we'd drunk mossy
cold, rust-flecked water
from the bottom of the well.

WILLIAM MATHEWS

DELLA'S BUS

We're lined up in the hollow,
fat paper cut-outs in snowsuits. Trees
scratch black on the rising yellow,
and the other way, it's the not-quite blue
of crows. Deep January. We're waiting for Della,
rocking and squeaking, our lashes stuck together
like starpoints. Breath through red wool
has given us white Valentines for mouths.

At minus forty, the phone lines are
giving up their secrets: words fall straight
into the air. We listen to Mrs. Bluedorn, she's
telling her stitches to the party-line—
at the sound of "hysterectomy," we all
parade around on our heels. Mr. Yutne drives by
with thumping tires, they're frozen, he waves.
We wonder how long people live.

The lake cracks and booms. Here's Della,
her bus is orange with double headlights.
Only Clara Ring gets on before we do—
she sits at the back, too poor to have friends,
her family has goats, and an outhouse. She
has breasts. We huddle together in the middle seats.
Della frowns in the rear-view mirror, and always,
from the back, that pull. It makes us shiver.

KATHY CALLAWAY

SUMMER WEEKEND

It was the heat I think.
Boys I had sat beside all year
began to capture the cats
mostly strays I suppose
slow from lack of water
tricked by bits of fish
and they took them
behind the school
to a corner of the playground
where they had rigged a cage
four by four of wire mesh.
The whole steamy weekend they hunted.
There were about a dozen in the end
without water or food or shade

and in some ritual they had devised
they would surround the cage
and pee and pee in great yellow arcs.
None of the cats moved very much.
I watched from my place behind the fence.
I don't know why
they finally set them loose.

FLORENCE GROSSMAN

TO BURY A HORSE IN TEXAS

Thirty years old, the only horse
we owned died on Christmas Eve;
my mother saw the feet flashing
in the winter light
trying to touch ground. She cried.
Father shot three times,
did not know the spot so somewhere
between the eyes it
took the hint, gave up.

What do you do with a horse dead
for Christmas, the renderers closed
till New Year, flies catching the scent?
You and all your brothers dig
while the sun shines, you watch
its side where a last breath
gathers through the day.

The yellow earth opened beside it.
We dug close to drag it less far.
We covered it. For Christmas
that year I got boots and guns
to play at cowboy.

In the white night a horse floats in awful
phosphorescence. The mad child rides
brandishing silver guns with the message
in red on the barrels: *Kill him for me,*
I am so young.

BIN RAMKE

SPRING SNOW

Here comes the powdered milk I drank
as a child, and the money it saved.
Here come the papers I delivered,
the spotted dog in heat that followed me home

and the dogs that followed her.
Here comes a load of white laundry
from basketball practice, and sheets
with their watermarks of semen.

And here comes snow, a language
in which no word is ever repeated,
love is impossible, and remorse . . .
Yet childhood doesn't end,

but accumulates, each memory
knit to the next, and the fields
become one field. If to die is to lose
all detail, then death is not

so distinguished, but a profusion
of detail, a last gossip, character
passed wholly into fate and fate
in flecks, like dust, like flour, like snow.

WILLIAM MATHEWS

3
THINGS

1

Paper clips, rubber bands, a book of matches, these small things that go about the daily business of their lives— most people would never think of them as the subjects of poetry. But as walls have ears and pillows have secrets, each of these things has its own story. It has been places and has done things. For the poet it's a matter of tuning in, of holding the spool of thread until we have heard what it has to say. Look long enough at a pencil and the poem will begin.

THE UNWRITTEN

Inside this pencil
crouch words that have never been written
never been spoken
never been thought

they're hiding

they're awake in there
dark in the dark
hearing us
but they won't come out
not for love not for time not for fire

even when the dark has worn away
they'll still be there
hiding in the air
multitudes in days to come may walk through them
breathe them
be none the wiser

what script can it be
that they won't unroll
in what language
would I recognize it
would I be able to follow it
to make out the real names
of everything

maybe there aren't
many
it could be that there's only one word
and it's all we need
it's here in this pencil

every pencil in the world
is like this

W. S. MERWIN

What words are crouching inside your pencil? What do they want to say? If there were only one word, what would it be? And what about the paper it's going to write on? Josephine Miles tells its story.

PAPER

This soft paper
Asks a soft answer,
Asks to think of mohair
Nimble
Silky
Poised, eyes lidded
In a soft light.
And the wire-lines of the paper
Carry its question
Literally
From word to word.

And your paper? Does it ask a soft answer? Or is it itching for some astounding message to the world?

By looking outside ourselves, by touching something outside ourselves, we can come to ourselves. By allowing the outside to move inside, we can make that kind of discovery that is a poem. Donald Justice begins with a stone.

THINGS

Stone

Hard, but you can polish it.
Precious, it has eyes. Can wound.
Would dance upon water. Sinks.
Stays put. Crushed, becomes a road.

Pillow

Mine to give, mine to offer
No resistance. Mine
To receive you, mine to keep
The shape of our nights.

Mirror

My former friend, my traitor.
My too easily broken.
My still to be escaped from.

Wall

To support this roof.
To stand up. To take
Such weight in the knees . . .
To keep the secret.
To envy no cloud.

Clock

These quiet hands, their gestures,
These circles drawn upon air.
And the whiteness of the face
That attends the unspoken.
This listening of the deaf.

The poet reminds us. Yes, a stone dances on water. Yes, it stays put. These are *his* associations with stone. What comes to *your* mind when you consider stone? If you hold a particular stone in your hand, a smooth white stone from the seashore, a flat black one from the lake, the associations to stone will begin to tumble out. *Pillow*, for Donald Justice, becomes a kind of love poem. The mirror, the wall, the clock are transformed into more than themselves. Why does the wall envy no cloud? Why is the mirror a traitor? Which details clue us in to the personality of *Clock*? What could you tell us about a blackboard? a piece of chalk? an eraser? What do they say to each other after you've left the classroom?

The following poems by students are about some of the things they've considered.

PAINTBRUSH

It moves
from one mind's
imagination
to the next
letting pictures
in our eyes
come out
showing the world
a dream.

JILL FOOTLICK

RED THREAD

Sews things
Bows things
Ties things
Flies things
Fixes, mends
Some clothes depend
On red thread

LANE COGGIN

CANDLE

A brave soldier
it sacrifices itself as an adversary
to darkness.
It stands straight
in the line
of fire.

LAWRENCE BELFER

One way for you to begin is with a treasure hunt in which you actually set about gathering the nuts and bolts of your life—"treasures" you've always taken for granted—obvious things, everyday kinds of things. It's finding the freshness (creating the freshness by naming it, which only language can do) in the so-called ordinary world that makes the ordinary world not ordinary at all. Here are some suggestions for a beginning collection:

thimble	nail	string
needle	band-aid	old bottle
wine cork	battery	button
spool of white thread	chewed stubby pencil	dice
spool of black thread	broken shoelace	purple crayon
ticket stub	small box	fork
bead	pocket knife	safety pin

Choose one you think you could work with. Look at it as if you were making a kind of exploration. Touch it. Become its friend. Allow yourself to be open to the thimbleness of thimble. In Donald Justice's poem, the wall is confident. The stone has many faces. The clockness of clock is its composure. Think of these questions:

What does it consider its strength?
What does it consider its vulnerability?
Is it cautious or headstrong?
What might it be embarrassed by?
Is it flamboyant or unassuming?
What might it be jealous of?
What might it feel guilty about?
Can it be trusted?

Let it tell you about itself in its own words. Make us see it as itself and more than itself. Remind us. After you have written about one, try another and perhaps another. When you have had enough of the real world, you might make real, as Lawrence Raab does,

THE INVISIBLE OBJECT

Held toward light
in the shape of your hands
it's clearer than water,
clearer than glass,
than air.

Against the sky, sometimes
it's red, sometimes it's blue.
Set in the grass in your garden
the bees stumble through it.

Looking closely
inside there's always another day
where your life could be.
Yet it has nothing to do
with dreams that change
when you change your mind.

On a table at night it becomes
the center of your house,
a small fire in a darkened room,
and the silence bends toward it
and touches it with one finger.

Lost for days it appears
suddenly
in a pile of old hats.

No reason to be there,
no reason to be anywhere else.

2

Now let's move outside to the small things of the
natural world, like a leaf or a blade of grass. John Moffitt
tells us how to look.

TO LOOK AT ANY THING

To look at any thing,
If you would know that thing,
You must look at it long:
To look at this green and say

'I have seen spring in these
Woods,' will not do—you must
Be the thing you see:
You must be the dark snakes of
Stems and ferny plumes of leaves,
You must enter in
To the small silences between
The leaves,
You must take your time
And touch the very peace
They issue from.

Sometimes we're better able to direct our attention to
something small, something particular, like a ray of light, rather
than to something overwhelming like a sunset. Or we're better
able to grasp, literally and figuratively, something we can hold
in our hands. The following poems are by students who looked
long and hard before they were able to go beyond the boundary
of stone and shell.

STONE

I hold a rock
with its black
sky and white clouds.
As I stare at it
I lose my distance.

OLIVER CHUBB

SHELL

Where is the
            creature
Who left us
His house
Like the anonymous poet?

RACHEL SCHINDLER

The center of each of these poems is an implied comparison—the shell to a poem, the rock to a universe. How is a shell
like a poem? a rock like a universe? What is the comparison in
William Carlos Williams' poem

THE WILDFLOWER

Black eyed susan
rich orange
round the purple core

the white daisy
is not enough

Crowds are white
as farmers
who live poorly

But you
are rich
in savagery—

Arab
Indian
dark woman.

These are some possibilities from which you might
want to choose:

a puddle iced over	a snowflake	a nest
a mosquito	a cattail	a shell
a moth	a pine cone	a stone
a housefly	a weed	a leaf
a grain of sand	a wildflower	the froth of a wave
tracks in the snow	a bird's feather	an ant
the bark of a tree	a dandelion	a spider web

"You must take your time." See the moth in its own way.
Think about its color, its motion, its stillness, the light in
which it lives. What can it be compared to? What does it remind you of? How does it make you feel?

One of the pitfalls in writing about nature is the
temptation to fall into clichés, those overworked words and
phrases that direct our minds along laid out tracks. Because
we've heard them so many times, they no longer mean very
much. Reading about a puffy cloud that floats or drifts or
sails, we discover nothing new. But to see something for what
it is and for what it could be, to know what it thinks about
itself and the cattail growing beside it, will help you write
about it as it has never been written about before.

After you have written your poem, you might want to read *Snow* by Laura Gilpin, *Note* by William Stafford, and *Stone* by Charles Simic. In each case, the snow, the stone, the ordinary things, are themselves and more. But before something can be more than itself, it must be truly itself, truly stone, truly snow. Laura Gilpin reminds us of what we know about snow, each flake separate, distinct, how it transforms a hillside. What else might she be writing about? What else might the stone be for Charles Simic? the little things for William Stafford?

SNOW

Each flake of snow
so separate
so distinct

yet in the morning
the hillside is a
solid field of white.

LAURA GILPIN

NOTE

straw, feathers, dust—
little things

but if they all go one way,
that's the way the wind goes

WILLIAM STAFFORD

STONE

Go inside a stone
That would be my way.
Let someone else become a dove
Or gnash with a tiger's tooth.
I am happy to be a stone.

From the outside the stone is a riddle:
No one knows how to answer it.
Yet within, it must be cool and quiet
Even though a cow steps on it full weight
Even though a child throws it in a river;
The stone sinks, slow, unperturbed

To the river bottom
Where the fishes come to knock on it
And listen.

I have seen sparks fly out
When two stones are rubbed,
So perhaps it is not dark inside after all;
Perhaps there is a moon shining
From somewhere, as though behind a hill—
Just enough light to make out
The strange writings, the star-charts
On the inner walls.

CHARLES SIMIC

3

Because the natural world is so full of wonder and even the smallest things have their own kind of perfection, it's understandable how nature would provide the backdrop for and the subject of many poems. But it takes a special vision and a special kind of looking to see the strength and the grace, as Ted Kooser does, of a beer bottle.

BEER BOTTLE

In the burned-
out highway
ditch the throw-

away beer
bottle lands
standing up

unbroken,
like a cat
thrown off

of a roof
to kill it,
landing hard

and dazzled
in the sun
right side up;

sort of a
miracle.

So, too, in the following poems by students, we are
surprised to discover the poetry in the life of a mothball, a
telephone book, a bottle cap, broken glass.

AMIDST THE COATS

in the cold dark
reaches

of a closet
only

the odor
of mothballs

embraces
the torn

and tattered pages
of a telephone book.

LARRY ROBERTS

BOTTLE CAP

In the swirling
ocean

quite near
the shore

lay a small bottle cap
its dented edges
forming shapes

in the sand.
It sparkles
under water.

MARO CHERMAYEFF

BROKEN GLASS

Showering confusion
like a cat on a piano
it captures and dazzles the rainbow
    rays of the sun.

MAGGIE ROSEN

"Embraces" is the word that changes the nature of mothballs and clues us in to the closet affair. Why is the word "reaches" interesting? What lifts the bottle cap out of the rusty, cut-your-foot-on, variety? What is the switch on "dazzles"? Again, keeping the scale fairly small, try to find the beauty in something that would not ordinarily be thought beautiful. You might consider,

an inside-out umbrella	the shell of a bullet
old shoes	the smell of disinfectant
a newspaper blowing down the street	a garbage dump
smoke stacks	a cracked cup and saucer
rust	a furnace
a gas pump	coal
a bat	an oil slick
a deserted lot	mud

Give us second thoughts. Change its life as we ordinarily know it.
    After you've written your poem, you might want to read Norman MacCaig's *Frogs*, David Wagoner's *The Death of a Crane Fly*, and Denise Levertov's *To the Snake*. Although MacCaig's frog doesn't become a prince, there is a kind of princeliness about it. It has its own kind of beauty. How does David Wagoner change the death of the crane fly? How does Denise Levertov make us re-think snake?

FROGS

Frogs sit more solid
Than anything sits. In mid-leap they are
Parachutists falling
In a free fall. They die on roads
With arms across their chests and
Heads high.

I love frogs that sit
Like Buddha, that fall without
Parachutes, that die
Like Italian tenors.

Above all, I love them because,
Pursued in water, they never
Panic so much that they fail
To make stylish triangles
With their ballet dancer's
Legs.

NORMAN MacCAIG

THE DEATH OF A CRANE FLY

It falls from the air
Stricken, spiralling
Lamely, already dying,
Its arched frail inch
Of body trailing
The long disjointed-seeming
Legs out of sunlight
Onto the pond's dark water
Where swiftly a water strider
Clings to it, rippling
And skimming away with it over
reflections of yellow leaves,
Holding one amber
Lace-ribbed, lifeless wing
Aloft (a small sail
Disappearing among the quiet
Inlets of milfoil)
As bouyantly as a lover.

DAVID WAGONER

TO THE SNAKE

Green Snake, when I hung you round my neck
and stroked your cold, pulsing throat
     as you hissed to me glinting
arrowy gold scales, and I felt
     the weight of you on my shoulders,
and the whispering silver of your dryness
     sounded close at my ears —

Green Snake—I swore to my companions that certainly
    you were harmless! But truly
I had no certainty, and no hope, only desiring
    to hold you, for that joy,
                which left
a long wake of pleasure, as the leaves moved
and you faded into the pattern
of grass and shadows, and I returned
smiling and haunted, to a dark morning.

DENISE LEVERTOV

4

For the most part we've been browsing around inside/
outside things different from the keepsakes in Carl Sandburg's

STREET WINDOW

The pawn-shop man knows hunger,
And how far hunger has eaten the heart
Of one who comes with an old keepsake.
Here are wedding rings and baby bracelets,
Scarf pins and shoe buckles, jeweled garters,
Old-fashioned knives with inlaid handles,
Watches of old gold and silver,
Old coins worn with finger marks.
They tell stories.

Write a poem about something old, a kind of keepsake.
Keepsake means, "Anything kept, or given to be kept, for the
sake of the giver." It might be one of the things Carl Sandburg
mentions in his poem or you might want to take a look around
your house or your grandmother's house to find something that
has a history, real or invented. Perhaps there is an old leather-
bound book, a key, or an old picture in an old frame. It might
be a handkerchief carried at a wedding or a family *Bible* with all
of the names inscribed. It might be an old tea cup or cocoa pot,
an old pistol, a belt buckle, a watch chain, an unusual piece of
jewelry, not necessarily valuable but precious—something that
means something to somebody, to you. Let it tell you the story

of itself or tell us the story, as Laura Gilpin does, of her great-grandmother's wristwatch.

MY GREAT-GRANDMOTHER'S WRISTWATCH

My great-grandmother's wristwatch still keeps
perfect time. My mother said, as far as she can
remember, it's always kept perfect time, when her
grandmother had it, when her mother had it, and when
she had it. But a few years ago it stopped and none
of the jewelers she took it to could fix it. They
said it was too old and they didn't have parts for
it. My mother saved it for sentimental value and
it sat around the house for a couple of years.

Then she gave it to me because I needed a watch and
she said I could have it if I could get it fixed.
Most jewelers wouldn't even look at it, it was so
old. Finally in New York I found a watchmaker who
specialized in antiques. He cleaned and polished
my great-grandmother's watch and now it looks as
good as new. He said it's a fine piece of machinery.
He said it just needed some minor adjustments. He
said it works perfectly. He said it should last
another lifetime.

The rhythm of the poem is very much the rhythm, the pace,
the breathing of a story, but notice where the lines end, how
each line carries the story further down the page so that you
can almost ask, "What next? What next?"

4
SIGNS

Among the things we might not ordinarily think of as the subjects of poetry are things like letters and numbers, geometric figures and marks of punctuation, which if you let them, lead lives of their own. For instance, take another look at the numbers. You have never seen a zero before. What is it? This is what May Swenson sees.

CARDINAL IDEOGRAMS

0   A mouth. Can blow or breathe,
    be a funnel, or Hello.

1   A grass blade or a cut.

2   A question seated. And a proud
    bird's neck.

3   Shallow mitten for two-fingered hand.

4   Three-cornered hut
    on one stilt. Sometimes built
    so the roof gapes.

5   A policeman. Polite.
    Wearing visored cap.

6   O unrolling,
    tape of ambiguous length
    on which is written the mystery
    of everything curly.

7   A step,
    detached from its stair.

8   The universe in diagram:
    A cosmic hourglass.
    (Note enigmatic shape,
    absence of any valve of origin,
    how end overlaps beginning.)
    Unknotted like a shoelace
    and whipped back and forth,
    can serve as a model of time.

9   Lorgnette for the right eye.
    In England or if you are Alice
    the stem is on the left.

10   A grass blade or a cut
     companioned by a mouth
     Open? Open. Shut? Shut.

What would you write about 11? 111? 13? 99? 100?

Begin by trying a few letters. Go back in your own mind to how you might have seen these strange marks before you learned how to read or write. How would a primitive person have seen them? What is the letter Y—a fork in the road? a tree? Stare at the letter until it loses its meaning as a letter and it becomes a shape. Make us see what you see. Each sign has its own truth. These are some of the notions of students.

THE NEW AND SELECTED ALPHABET

B   Big Bimbo pouting out your abdomen

C   Blue-green holds me in her shore

D   Too fat—don't fall down

E   Shivers up the spine under
      the thin orange sweater

H   Passive soothing hallways

J   Waits for the fish

K   Marches through a square somewhere

Q   Cuddles her child in fat arms

R   Strolls through his palace
on a Sunday afternoon

S   Tickles the roof of my mouth

T   Good athlete, good balance
Skips English, comes early to math

U   A roller coaster
Zoom down one side in your sleek car
Roll slowly up the other

V   The fatal blow of the axe

W   Creeps through the swamp

X   Doesn't Won't Can't Shouldn't

Y   Makes love in the early morning

Z   Breaks glass

2

Now that you've warmed up on one-liners, try a longer poem about a letter. Look again, very hard, until the letter disappears and all that you see is the shape. Write down, as fast as you can without stopping, *all of the things* you can think of about that letter, even if what you write seems disconnected or strange. Some of it will hang together. Some of the lines will be more interesting than others. Choose the lines you like best for your poem. Sometimes what you've written will work just the way it is except for one or two words that may have to be taken out or changed.

These are some poems by students. Why is the title, "Let X Be," an interesting one? What makes the rhythm of "O"?

LET X BE

Let X be what?
Whatever the problem calls for.
How about asking X what it would like
    to be?
Why it doesn't have feelings or color?
How do you know? What do you suppose
    it does all period
    sitting on the blackboard?
It does what the teacher tells it.

SAM CHAPMAN

O

O is blue like
The blue O sea
For the sea is blue
For the sea is O

O is blue like
The blue O sky
For the sky is blue
For the sky is O

O is blue like
The blue O everything
For everything is O
For everything is blue

DAVID FLAXMAN

3

Imagine now, the lives of parallel lines, the confusion
of the ellipsis . . . , how the apostrophe sings in mid air. Consider the possibilities of the parts of speech. If you had a choice,
which would you prefer to be, a verb or a pronoun? The following poems are by students. Some of them began by the student
writing down everything that came into his or her head and then
making selections, like "The Hyphen." Some of them came from
a flash impression, like "Comma." Notice that the comma "sits."
An exclamation point would stand . . . off balance? Often, when
we write about something abstract, we come to feelings we might

not otherwise have expressed. We come to them, so to speak, through the back door.

COMMA

On a blue gray day
a comma sat on the edge of a cliff
        staring into the sea
thinking of famous interruptions
        it had made.

AMY BARASCH

CIRCLE

Shh . . .
No one knows
the angles — starts . . .
— stops — slashes
falling off ice cream cones
glowing on reindeer faces
bouncing on basketball courts.
Calm, controlled, assuring
Me? Have I got you fooled.

MARYA COHEN

HYPHEN

A hyphen lets things stay close,
yet not touching.
It separates the best of friends
but not forever.
It separates the vice
        from the president
the mother from her in-laws.
It never makes grand entrances,
just squeezes in with the crowd.
The hyphen is a mingler
not a leader or a follower.

KATE FEIFFER

CUBE

A place for everyone
    to be
to have his own space
with the security of someone
just around the corner.
When the world is turned
a new space emerges.

LILI SCHLOSSBERG

ELLIPSIS

The ellipsis is dreaming
Entering a new world
Letting its imagination run wild
Or maybe it's sleeping late
    on a rainy day
    or a Sunday afternoon.
It's sitting in its brother's chair.
The book slips out of its hand.

WENDY RISS

Write a poem about a geometric figure, a part of speech, a number, a mark of punctuation, or any other sign—the asterisk, the equal sign, the plus, the minus. Take a new look at something familiar. Think of these questions:

If it had a voice, how would it speak?
Does it whisper or shout?
Does it use long words or short?
Does it have a great deal of patience? a sense of humor?
Who are its friends?
How does it spend its spare time?
What does it dream?

To get started, you might begin with a first line like,

So this is what it's like to be a . . .

Talk in the voice of your subject. A period would speak very differently and have very different things to say from a question mark; so, too, a circle and a square. Another way to begin might be as some of the oldest and truest stories,

Once upon a time . . .

What can you remind us of that we already know? What can
you tell us that we have never heard before?

Here are some more poems that have to do with
letters, numbers, marks of punctuation, geometric figures,
and parts of speech.

THE POSSESSIVE CASE

Your father's mustache
My brother's keeper
La plume de ma tante
Le monocle de mon oncle
His Master's Voice
Son of a bitch
Charley's Aunt
Lady Chatterley's Lover
    The Prince of Wales
    The Duchess of Windsor
    The Count of Monte Cristo
    The Emperor of Ice Cream
    The Marquis de Sade
    The Queen of the Night
        Mozart's Requiem
        Beethoven's Ninth
        Bach's B-Minor Mass
        Schubert's Unfinished
        Krapp's Last Tape
        Custer's Last Stand
        Howard's End
        Finnegan's Wake
            The March of Time
            The Ides of March
            The Auroras of Autumn
            The Winter of our discontent
            The hounds of spring
            The Hound of Heaven
        Dante's Inferno
        Virgil's Aeneid
        Homer's Iliad
    The Fall of the City
    The Decline of the West
    The Birth of a Nation

The Declaration of Independence
The ride of Paul Revere
The Pledge of Allegiance
The Spirit of '76
    The Age of Reason
    The Century of the Common Man
    The Psychopathology of Everyday Life
        Portnoy's Complaint
        Whistler's Mother
        The Sweetheart of Sigma Chi
        The whore of Babylon
        The Bride of Frankenstein
        The French Lieutenant's Woman
           A Room of One's Own
           Bluebeard's Castle
           Plato's Cave
           Santa's Workshop
           Noah's ark
           The House of Seven Gables
        The Dance of the Seven Veils
        Anitra's Dance
        The Moor's Pavanne
        My Papa's Waltz
    Your father's mustache

LISEL MUELLER

NOUNS

Nouns are precise, they wear
the boots of authority;

Nouns are not easily pleased.
Nouns are assured, they know

Whom to precede and whom to follow,
They know what dependence means,

That touchstone of happiness;
They need no apologist.

When nouns fall to disuse, and die,
Their bones do not coalesce.

Such absences implicate
No person, no place, no thing.

CHARLES WRIGHT

PRUDENT TRIANGLE

Once upon a time there was a triangle.
It had three sides.
The fourth it kept hidden
In its burning center.

By day it climbed its three peaks
And admired its center.
At night it rested
In one of its three angles.

Each dawn it watched its three sides
Turn into three fiery wheels
And vanish in the blue of never return.

It took its fourth side
Embraced it and broke it three times
To hide it again in its old place

And again it had only three sides

And again it climbed each day
To its three peaks
And admired its center
While at night it rested
In one of its angles.

VASCO POPA
(Translated by Charles Simic)

THE LOCUS OF A POINT

I sleep
in the swing of the ball
away from the sun.

I wake
as it turns to light,
and move with the arc
of the day.
What is that ray
connects me
to the center?
Why does the whole
wheel shine
sometimes?

Rays shake and shimmer,
slacken, tauten,
sing.
The ball revolves.

Though circumscribed
I dance
in many circles.

LILLIAN MORRISON

CONJUGATION OF THE VERB, "TO HOPE"

I hoped
— the night came anyway

I hoped
— the night came anyway

Is this the way to
do it?

No. Begin again.

I hoped
today.

I will still hope,
tomorrow.

One day,
I will risk everything.

LOU LIPSITZ

from House-Marks*

THE CHEVRON

This is my sign, the pitch
of my tent on low ground.
It is the march up the mountain
and the march down. It is
a crossroads without a choice.
It is my past and my future
leaning together like cornstalks
after the rain. This broken
stick confers no honor,
but it has marked me.
It has stolen the comfort
of a bare sleeve.

THE WINDLASS

In me, opposites face each other
like poker players drawn to the table
yet holding their cards to themselves.
Spades, diamonds, hearts, clubs.
The chips meet in the middle.
One man deals the cards, clockwise,
into four piles, their backs
patterned like four turtles floating
in a slow eddy. The players are skillful
and cautious; the money rises and falls
gently in front of them. It is late,
but no one moves to leave. Finally,
they notice that all of them are
losing. The game grows silent, except
for the creak of the table, turning.

CONRAD HILBERRY

*"House-marks were, at first, private signs of peasant proprietors, and their use
was originally confined to their holdings, all moveable property which was distinguished by the holdings-mark" (Rudolph Koch, *The Book of Signs*).

THE BALLAD OF THE WHEEL

so that's what it's like to be a wheel
so that's what it's like to be tied to one of its spokes
while the rim screeches while the hub grinds
so that's what it's like to have the earth and heaven
    confused
to speak of the stars on the road
of stones churning in the icy sky
to suffer as the wheel suffers
to bear its unimaginable weight

if only it were a honing wheel
I would have sparks to see by
if only it were a mill stone
I would have bread to keep my mouth busy
if only it were a roulette wheel
my left eye would watch its right dance in it

so that's what it's like
to be chained to the wounded rib of a wheel
to move as the hearse moves
to move as the lumber truck moves
down the mountains at night

*

what do you think of my love
while the wheel turns

I think of the horse out in front
how the snowflakes are caught in his mane
how he shakes his beautiful blindfolded head
I think how in the springtime
two birds are pulling us along as they fly
how one bird is a crow
and the other a swallow
I think how in the summertime
there's no one out there
except the clouds in the blue sky
except the dusk in the blue sky
I think how in autumn
there's a man harnessed out there
a bearded man with the bit stuck in his mouth
a hunchback with a blanket over his shoulder
hauling the wheel
heavy as earth

*

don't you hear I say don't you hear
the wheel talk as it turns

I have the impression that it's hugging me closer
that it has maternal instincts
that it's telling me a bedtime story
that it knows the way home
that I grit my teeth just like my father

I have the impression
that it whispers to me
how all I have to do
to stop its turning
is to hold my breath

CHARLES SIMIC

COMPUTING DISTANCE

It is a matter of seeing clearly.
Knowing more than one point called beginning
And the other we are afraid to name.
Remember how it went in grammar school:
If A left New York at 10, moving West
And B from San Francisco headed East
With a different time and greater speed
(Tail winds not entering the problem . . .)
Compute their arrival to four places:
But what if they met? Say, over Chicago?
Or one side of the equation slipped
Across the equal sign for a visit?
What remains would be positive. Minus
The icy fingers you did not count on.

SANFORD PINSKER

5
IMAGE

Image is the snapshot we retain years later, or the morning after. It's the concrete picture, the re-run, the mind conjures up. No way of knowing ahead of time what you'll extract from a day at the beach—the radio blaring on the next blanket, the smell of suntan oil—but it will be a moment of reality closed off as small as a picture than can open up the whole day. We think in images. We remember in images, in particulars. They are the information we have received through our senses, the partnership between body and mind.

Mention baking, and while one person might smell bread, another might smell chocolate chip cookies. Take radish, for instance. Think of the radishness of radish, the possibilities of radish, the color and condition of a particular radish. What is the picture that comes to *your* mind? Is it the radish just picked and washed, drops of water still on the surface, the root intact, the green leaves not yet wilted? Or is it one radish crowded among many slightly faded in a plastic supermarket bag? Perhaps it's the radish painted as still-life with green pepper beside a white bowl. Or the radish as embellishment to tuna fish. Or the radish, tiny, perfect, cut to the shape of a rose, glistening in a martini. That is the look of radish and we have only just begun. There is, of course, the taste of radish, the texture, not to mention the sound which, if you listen carefully, is closer to carrot than to celery, and the smell, faint, nevertheless, evident.

In the William Carlos Williams poem that follows, we are on the verge of tasting plums.

THIS IS JUST TO SAY

I have eaten
the plums
that were in
the icebox

and which
you were probably
saving
for breakfast

Forgive me
they were delicious
so sweet
and so cold

Although the poet starts in the particular place of plums, the poem goes further than an image of cold plums. It's a note of apology that's not really an apology. That it's an adventure with forbidden fruit makes the plums even sweeter. Why is the word, "saving," important enough to be on a line by itself?

The next poem by a student starts in Swenson's Ice Cream Parlor. Again, it is more than an image of taste. What makes it work is that someone is having the experience and is making another kind of apology.

SWENSON'S

Not much
to be sorry for
        the creamy coldness
        warmed my tastebuds
        I felt happy
I only apologize
to my waistline
        My mouth and my spoon
        though
        have no regrets.

ERICA SCHWARTZ

Each of the following poems by students creates another kind of sense image. Each recalls an impression, a small moment caught and held—

Of Sound—

> Among
> silence
> blue
>
> whispers
> travel
> quietly

LAURA MODLIN

> Listen
> the birds are explaining
> why
> we hit the ground
> right after takeoff

JEFF THROPE

Of Touch—

CINQUAIN ON SWIMMING

> Cool blue
> and I am calm,
> so sensuous a blue
> that now I am in rhythm with
> the tides.

AMY BODIAN

OLD PEOPLE

> You let go fast
> Holding hands with a skeleton
> The lifeless drop of the fingers
> The blue veins protruding
> The faded freckles blending into the loose skin
> You let go fast

MINDY MOROWITZ

Of Sight—

SLED

The old
Flexible Flyer
leans against
the garage wall
the blades rusted
yet smooth
the remembrance
of its speed
on the pure white snow.

JON HARRIS

After it rains
the branches grow
waterberries.

RICKY GOTTLIEB

Of Smell—

DINER

Hamburgers frying
Greasy cheese
And greasy spoons
Two blacks one regular to go
Bubble gum is 5¢ now
And the *Daily News* is all sold out

SHELLY TALISMAN

MY BROTHER

home from college
I kiss him hello
he smells like luggage
and Noxema Shaving Cream
his jacket
like the Men's Department
when he walks into the kitchen
his eyes light up
he must smell dinner

KATHY SPIZER

In each of the images there is a relationship between the speaker and his or her material. Sometimes the speaker is off-stage, sometimes part of the action. But always, we sense the voice. "Finding a voice," says the poet Seamus Heaney, "means that you can get your own feeling into your own words and that your words have the feel of you about them . . ."

Write a poem that creates a sense image. Remind us of something we have almost forgotten or tell us something we have never heard before. In order to be able to do this, you'll have to put yourself in the place of that memory, that sense experience. In your mind's eye, you will have to taste again the stale coffee and the greasy doughnuts, hear the water squishing in your sneakers, smell the clean sheets and fancy soap, feel the blade of the razor. To get started you might think of

> the touch that sets your teeth on edge
> the smell that makes you feel nostalgic
> the taste that curls your tongue
> the sight that makes you shudder
> the sound you would know if you woke in the middle
> of the night

Begin with substance. You might try as a first line one of the following which you may or may not discard once the poem is written.

> Sometimes I hear
> Yesterday I saw
> The hair in my nose
> This morning I watched
> Listen
> If I blink
> I still taste
> The balance in my ears
> Between my thumb and forefinger
> My time of day

Let the image that comes to your head be the guidepost, the first step on the path. Keep the language simple and straight. Don't let it get in the way of the picture or of your feelings. Try to let the experience of the image dictate the language.

2

Although we might experience a predominant sensation, such as heat, usually we experience things through several of our senses at the same time. Which of the senses are involved in this poem by Robert Bly?

DRIVING TO TOWN LATE TO MAIL A LETTER

It is a cold and snowy night. The main street is deserted.
The only things moving are swirls of snow.
As I lift the mailbox door, I feel its cold iron.
There is a privacy I love in this snowy night.
Driving around, I will waste more time.

And in these by students—

LATE SUMMER

Often I remember
those few
crisp days
water
sparkling beneath
light weight silver canoes

ALISON SHOTZ

HOT BATH

I watch the swirls of steam
curling to the ceiling.
My tired eyelids begin to droop
and my muscles melt into water.

JONO STEINBERG

None of these poems starts from a dramatic or spectacular experience, but each of them starts in a particular place. Two are written in the present tense so that we almost go along for the ride with Robert Bly . . . or take the hot bath. The third is a recollection. Which details make the poems vivid? What do they reveal about the speakers?

Write a poem that involves more than one of your senses. You might begin by putting yourself in a particular place. Perhaps you're sitting on a train or lying in the grass on a scratchy blanket. Perhaps it's late and you're in a strange house. Or perhaps it's very early and you're waiting on the corner for a bus. Write down everything you see, hear, smell, touch, taste. Keep to the dailiness of things. Examine all the details and then bring together those that will make it possible for us, too, to go to that place and to sense why you have brought us there.

3

In his book, *I Am a Camera*, Christopher Isherwood shows, as if through the eye of a camera, a series of vignettes that reveal pre-war Germany. To create a picture with words, a camera image, someone must be behind the camera. Someone must decide what to focus on and when to use a wide-angle lens. Someone must be the "eye" and the "I." Focusing your camera eye on one particular, or on several particulars, using one or more of your senses, create a concrete image or series of images that will make us feel one of the following sensations:

heat	slowness
dryness	speed
stillness	wetness
cleanness	cold
bouyancy	grey

Besides the talk of rain, what makes us feel the dryness in

THE FLOWER LADY

Farmers have planted twice and still no rain.
Top soil and seed blow across the road
as if wheat would grow from the sky.

The woman walks out again and again
with filled cooking pots
careful to spill equally on iris, mum
and the white flowers only she can name,
then returns to the house beating dust
from her clothes.

At the corner store the talk is rain
enough to grow cabbages.

SANDI PICCONE

In these poems by students, which details make concrete the abstractions of dryness, cold, and heat?

DRYNESS

Parched
the earth is
a jigsaw for miles.
The wind sweeps
a sheet of dust
swirling upward
and my vision wavers
in the rising
heat.

JOAN BARZILAY

COLDNESS

It is
a winter dream
dark and drafty
climbing
the grey painted stairs.
My breath
shows white
against the shadows.
I breathe
on my hands
and run my finger
along the smooth
icy wall.

CINDY HALPERN

HEAT

I used to watch my father
in the room with so much steam
I could hardly breathe.
He would lather his face
reach for the razor
and look in the foggy mirror
where I had written my name.

LESLIE MARSHALL

4

Another way to get at sense impressions is through color. Ordinarily, we think of color as something we can see, and offhand we can think of ten things that are white. Even if we are not in a forest, we can picture a dozen shades of green. Without holding it in our hands, we can see the difference between the red of a Delicious apple and the red of a McIntosh. But suppose color had a sound. What are the things that would *sound* red—a fire engine? a whistle? a slap in the face? What is the color of the sound of a bass drum? the color of a piccolo practicing scales? What is the color of the sound of silence? Consider for a moment that color has movement. If white sits still, how does blue move? or purple? Consider the color of the wind. If we say that the wind is grey, we have a sense of the kind of day it is, how fast the wind is moving. If we say, "Today the wind is green," or "Today the wind is red," we know how that day feels on our skin. The color *connotes* or suggests the impression. Wallace Stevens in his poem, *Disillusionment of Ten O'Clock*, writes of the colorlessness of the lives of people whose houses are haunted by only white night-gowns.

DISILLUSIONMENT OF TEN O'CLOCK

The houses are haunted
By white night-gowns.
None are green,
Or purple with green rings,
Or green with yellow rings,
Or yellow with blue rings.
None of them are strange,
With socks of lace
And beaded ceintures.
People are not going
To dream of baboons and periwinkles.
Only, here and there, an old sailor,
Drunk and asleep in his boots,
Catches tigers
In red weather.

Where do you imagine the sailor's dream takes place? How would you describe the weather?

The following are some student impressions of color.
Notice the use of verbs. Red does not walk slowly. Red
sprints. Silver lingers.

> Grey whispers to the dark
> Purple takes chances when others play it safe
> Yellow hums
> Silver lingers after a party
> Violet stays in church windows
> Maroon has secrets
> Orange leaps and jumps like a bagged cat
> Red sprints to make the light
> Brown smudges and melts
> Green is a gust of spearmint wind
> Blue has all the answers
> White is the poem that is never written
>
> CLASS POEM

Write a poem of color using different colors or one
color, involving one sense or several senses. If you write a poem
about grey, you might begin by thinking of all of the things that
look grey, sound grey, taste grey and make you feel grey. Let the
experience of grey come to you in its own words.

5

Images are by no means limited to the five senses. Think
of the sensations within your body that are triggered by fear, by
love, by pain, or by fatigue. Think of a body in terms of motion.
In the next poem by William Carlos Williams we can see, almost
as if it had been filmed, the step by step movement of the cat.

POEM

As the cat
climbed over
the top of

the jamcloset
first the right
forefoot

carefully
then the hind
stepped down

into the pit of
the empty
flowerpot

The motion is made clear by the particular details that the poet observes and by where the lines and the stanzas are broken. He sees this movement and this hesitation, this rhythm, and he has made it the rhythm of his poem. How much less we would see in the motion of the cat if it were written as a prose sentence, "As the cat climbed over the top of the jamcloset, first the right forefoot, carefully, then the hind stepped down into the pit of the empty flowerpot."

How many times have you gone through the motions in the following poems written by students:

MOVING ON

The bell spoke—
time to move on
to the next class.
Pile the books on top of each other.
Check to make sure they are all there
in the right order
biggest to smallest.
Sweep the pile of education from the desk.
Cradle it under your arm
as you would cradle a football
when you are moving through a field
playing a different game.

PETER BRUUN

SNOW SCENE

Hold it—
Feel the cold, wet
Powder on your
Bare fingers.

Pack it—
Your hands turn red as it
Becomes a sphere
A weapon

Throw it—
It hits your friend
Square in the face.
The cold runs deep.

Run for it.

JORDAN SYMONS

In Peter Bruun's poem, how does the comparison of the books and the ball help to make each of the actions more vivid? Why is *cradle* an effective word? Jordan Symons' poem has about it the feeling of an incident with the instructions as a kind of refrain. Steve Sanders' poem is also an incident with a beginning, a middle, and an end.

POEM

It is dusk
and I overlook a placid lake.
Suddenly a beautifully marked trout
leaps out
of the water, breaking
the silence
to grasp a mayfly. He returns
to his home.
The rings are gone.

Write a poem which creates an image of motion. Try to visualize the motion from beginning to end. Are there interruptions? switches? pauses? How would a mime perform it? Which motions would she exaggerate? See what someone else has forgotten to see when you try one of the following:

your sister brushing her hair
your brother learning to ride a two wheeler
the dog on a chain
the foul shot
the bloody nose
the merry-go-round
the hammock

walking a tightrope
blowing up a balloon
undoing a knot

For the most part, we have been looking at poems that
have created an image from a sense impression behind which is
the eye and the emotion of the observer. In the following poem
by David Wagoner, we see behind the image an idea as well as an
emotion; that is, the image stands for more than itself.

NOTE FROM BODY TO SOUL

Each word a rock
The size of a fist—
I throw them one by one
At the dark window

What is the emotion behind the poem? What is the idea that the
image embodies? Why is it called, *Note from Body to Soul*?
Among the poems that follow are images of sense and
motion and behind them, emotion and idea.

SPRUCE WOODS

It is so still
today that a
dipping bough means
a squirrel
has gone through

A. R. AMMONS

MARGINS

It is the middle of December.
At the table where we eat,
winter settles between us.
Soup is served with bread,
bread with butter. My daughter
licks the butter from her fingers
with a soft tongue, watching one
of us, then another. She gets up
and goes to the window. She licks
a black hole in the frozen glass.

MARGARET BARRINGER

THE BASE STEALER

Poised between going on and back, pulled
Both ways taut like a tightrope-walker,
Fingertips pointing the opposites,
Now bouncing tiptoe like a dropped ball
Or a kid skipping rope, come on, come on,
Running a scattering of steps sidewise,
How he teeters, skitters, tingles, teases,
Taunts them, hovers like an ecstatic bird,
He's only flirting, crowd him, crowd him,
Delicate, delicate, delicate, delicate—now!

ROBERT FRANCIS

VACATION

One scene as I bow to pour her coffee:—

Three Indians in the scouring drouth
huddle at a grave scooped in the gravel,
lean to the wind as our train goes by.
Someone is gone.
There is dust on everything in Nevada.

I pour the cream.

WILLIAM STAFFORD

IN MEMORIAM

On that stormy night
a top branch broke off
on the biggest tree in my garden.

It's still up there. Though its leaves
are withered black among the green
the living branches
won't let it fall.

NORMAN MacCAIG

WHITE

Carafe, compotier, sea shell, vase:
Blank spaces, white objects;
Luminous knots along the black rope.

*

The clouds, great piles of oblivion, cruise
Over the world, the wind at their backs
Forever. They darken whomever they please.

*

The angel, his left hand on your left shoulder;
The bones, in draped white, at the door;
The bed-sheets, the pillow-case; your eyes.

*

I write your name for the last time in this mist,
White breath on the windowpane,
And watch it vanish. No, it stays there.

*

White, and the leaf clicks; dry rock;
White, and the wave spills.
Dogwood, the stripe, headlights, teeth.

CHARLES WRIGHT

THE ODOR OF PEAR

No wind bends the branches of those trees
behind my eyes, way back past
any distance I've a name for.

Though tears begin to gather like the rain,
they cannot bend the leaves of those trees
behind my eyes, far back past

any distance I've a name for.
For I remember pears, globed
to rust and gold, that yellowjackets tunneled

to the end of heavy summer. They'll never
rot and fall: for now, once more,
for all my time, the deep

odor of pear drifts up
from any distance I've a name for.

WILLIAM HEYEN

BLACKBERRY EATING

I love to go out in late September
among the fat, overripe, icy, black blackberries
to eat blackberries for breakfast,
the stalks very prickly, a penalty
they earn for knowing the black art
of blackberry-making; and as I stand among them
lifting the stalks to my mouth, the ripest berries
fall almost unbidden to my tongue,
as words sometimes do, certain peculiar words
like *strengths* or *squinched*,
many-lettered, one-syllabled lumps,
which I squeeze, squinch open, and splurge well
in the silent, startled, icy, black language
of blackberry-eating in late September.

GALWAY KINNELL

6

PEOPLE

1

High on the list of fascinating pastimes is people-watching. Certain places are set aside, like park benches and buses, libraries, the steps of a museum or, perhaps, your own front porch or front window where you can spend an hour or so imagining the lives of strangers. What are the things that give people away? Notice a gesture. Listen to the pitch of a voice. Tune in to a remark. Was that an honest laugh, a real smile? Have those clothes been chosen to call attention. Look carefully. A person's whole life can be seen in his walk. These are the kinds of details that writers collect and store. "Poets," says Etheridge Knight, "are naturally meddlers. They meddle in other people's lives and they meddle in their own, always searching and loving and questioning and digging into this or that."

Try moving in close to someone you really know, some-one who has a history you can draw upon. You know the kind of work he does and how he feels about it. You know how he spends his spare time, even what he eats for breakfast. He may be of average height, weight and build, but what about him is characteristic or unique? Think about someone you know the way John Updike knows Flick Webb,

EX-BASKETBALL PLAYER

Pearl Avenue runs past the high-school lot,
Bends with the trolley tracks, and stops, cut off
Before it has a chance to go two blocks,
At Colonel McComsky Plaza. Berth's Garage
Is on the corner facing west, and there,
Most days, you'll find Flick Webb, who helps Berth out.

Flick stands tall among the idiot pumps—
Five on a side, the old bubble-head style,
Their rubber elbows hanging loose and low.
One's nostrils are two S's, and his eyes
An E and O. And one is squat, without
A head at all—more of a football type.

Once Flick played for the high-school team, the Wizards.
He was good: in fact, the best. In '46
He bucketed three hundred ninety points,
A county record still. The ball loved Flick.
I saw him rack up thirty-eight or forty
In one home game. His hands were like wild birds.

He never learned a trade, he just sells gas,
Checks oil, and changes flats. Once in a while,
As a gag, he dribbles an inner tube,
But most of us remember anyway.
His hands are fine and nervous on the lug wrench.
It makes no difference to the lug wrench, though.

Off work, he hangs around Mae's luncheonette.
Grease-gray and kind of coiled, he plays pinball,
Smokes those thin cigars, nurses lemon phosphates.
Flick seldom says a word to Mae, just nods
Beyond her face toward bright applauding tiers
Of Necco Wafers, Nibs, and Juju Beads.

Dribbling an inner tube, Flick becomes alive against the
backdrop of Berth's Garage. We've been filled in on his past. We
see him at work, off work. We know the way he moves. We can
picture his hands, "fine and nervous on the lug wrench." Flick
is the perfect name. What do you notice about the language?
What's the effect of words like "bucketed" and "rack up"?

Linda Pastan also knows Caroline, but she has chosen
only one detail to help us see her.

CAROLINE

She wore
her coming death
as gracefully
as if it were a coat
she'd learned to sew.
When it grew cold enough
she'd simply button it
and go.

In the Old Soldiers' Home, Ted Kooser doesn't distinguish one soldier from another. Rather, he singles out one characteristic that gives us an insight into the lives of all the soldiers.

OLD SOLDIERS' HOME

On benches in front of the Old Soldiers' Home
the old soldiers unwrap the pale brown packages
of their hands, folding the fingers back
and looking inside, then closing them up again
and gazing off across the grounds,
safe with the secret.

Although each soldier goes through the same motions, we know that each has his separate secret.

We're able to know Flick and Caroline and the old soldiers because the authors are responding to what they see. We sense that someone is behind the poem telling us. We sense the way the poets feel because of the details they have selected to show us. One of the ways they've made these details vivid is through the use of comparison—in this case, what we call a *simile*. Caroline's life is like a coat, Flick's hands like wild birds, the soldiers' hands like pale brown packages. When two things are compared, both of them become more striking. Our imagination takes off—How are they like wild birds? Why?

In each of these poems by students, a personality emerges not only through the use of telling detail, but because someone is telling it to us. Which are the comparisons that work best for you?

CLIFF COBB
Social Studies Teacher

He held the great weight
of his head
heavily
between thumb and forefinger
as if the knowledge it contained
would seep out
without his support.

CARL COLEMAN

sybil

When I saw her
I felt cold.
She entered
as the wind, chilling the air.
If she touched me
I, too, turned icy.
If I felt a warm spark
ignite inside
I knew it was something
I had to hide
for the wind had come
and frosted my world
with its bitter tinge.

RICKIE STREISAND

JOHN

He was like a jack-knife
smooth and blunt
until
he opened up
then— deadly.

CINDY HALPERN

MR. X

His head was like a snowman's
White and pale
With two black spots, color of charcoal
Out of which he saw
An almost invisible mouth
A long thin nose.
The difference was the glasses.
He always talked about the weather.

ELIZABETH DICKEY

HE

was like a fog, drifting in and out.
You knew he was there
but he couldn't be touched.
When the time came, it was
as if he had faded away. He's still
here sometimes, part of him
in a corner
maybe.

COLIN SUMMERS

Like the telephoto lens of a camera, zoom in to someone
you find interesting. Walk around him/her physically and emo-
tionally. Relatives are the ones we generally know a great deal
about. Try a grandparent, an aunt, an uncle, an impossible cousin.
A mother or a father may be too close. Try a casual friend or a
neighbor. You might be most comfortable with a stranger, someone you can invent by rearranging the characteristics of people
you know. Whoever you write about should touch you deeply in
some way. By seeing someone else, you can discover yourself.

Once you have that person in focus, write down all of his
or her physical details. Is there one that's dominant, someone's
hair, for instance, or the shape of a nose? Is there something it can
be compared to? You should know that person well enough to
know all or most of the following:

on which side his hair is parted
how she sits, stands, walks
his favorite time of day
a particular facial expression, a movement of the eyebrows

a distinctive gesture, a barely perceptible shrug of the
  shoulders
whether she can carry a tune
the movie he has seen three times
whether she takes one lump of sugar or two
his favorite flavor of ice cream
the question about her a nosy neighbor would ask
the secret that only you know

You won't use all of these details. You may not use any of
them, but they'll help to fix that person clearly in your mind
and to recall other things you know.

Write a poem about a person using only one detail, as
Linda Pastan does in *Caroline*, keeping in mind that one precisely chosen detail, one specific incident, can reveal a life. Or
line up your character at a particular time in a particular place
and include a series of details, one of them, perhaps, outstand-
ing, as John Updike does in *Ex-Basketball Player*. Remember
that this is not a report from a police blotter—male, thirty years
old, 5'10", brown hair, blue eyes, last seen wearing . . . but like a
police report will include only that information that is necessary
to complete the picture. Try to use a comparison to give your
picture more life. What you choose to tell us will make clear not
only what you see but how you feel about your subject.

After you've finished writing your poem, you might want
to read Stanley Plumly's poem about his father. We're given no
particulars about what the man looked like, but through a series of
comparisons that touch on where he was in his life, he comes to us
whole and clear.

SUCH COUNSELS

My father would always come
back from the barn
as if he had been in conference.
He had the farm in him the way
some men have pain.
Every night the feed, the one
thing to get him home straight.

Still, he was a one-armed man,
toting his bottle
like a book of hours.
And he could sleep standing.
Each year to kill those cattle
he had to drink a week in a day
to stay cold sober.

In the poems that follow, notice the observer as well as
the observed. Each poem is like a two-character story in which
there is an interaction between two people, the speaker one of
them. Although a poet may create a speaker (someone other
than himself who is doing the telling) in many contemporary
poems, the poet and the speaker are often so close they are
really one. The emotional stance of both characters is apparent
in the selection of the details and the questions which make us
try to sense some of the answers.

GRANDFATHER

You slept evenly, hardly rumpling the sheet.
Later, I thought of places in Tennessee. The green
leapt off those hills, you said, explaining
your apple-core eyes.
A white field rumpled your jaw at night,
growing its own winter
carefully, without waste of time.
Sometimes you counted acres
you never owned, over and over, on fingers
handcuffed with age; you squinted
hospital fern into trees. How could
I know your sorrow? It was so private,
locked behind your fine, half-Cherokee skull,
and almost over, your face
tangled as the map of a civilized country.

MAURA STANTON

THOSE WINTER SUNDAYS

Sundays too my father got up early
and put his clothes on in the blueblack cold,
then with cracked hands that ached
from labor in the weekday weather made
banked fires blaze. No one ever thanked him.

I'd wake and hear the cold splintering, breaking.
When the rooms were warm, he'd call,
and slowly I would rise and dress,
fearing the chronic angers of that house,

Speaking indifferently to him
who had driven out the cold
and polished my good shoes as well.
What did I know, what did I know
of love's austere and lonely offices?

ROBERT HAYDEN

THE NUN ON THE TRAIN

Riding on the train
through summer banks of stitchwort
and forget-me-not
    forget-me-not
        forget-me-not
a nun nods in the heat.
She cannot loosen her heavy black dress
or tight white chinstrap
so her cheeks turn pink.
What does she think,
behind softly moving lips,
of those thighs of miniskirted girls
flirting with the Italians across
the aisle?
    What does she think
of the woman glimpsed in a bikini
painting window frames?
        And what
does she think of
Roderick Random in my lap
and even of my new red shoes?

JUDY RAY

2

In olden days, the trade of a person, like a kind of identity, might determine his name; for instance, Silversmith or Carpenter. And although this way of naming has changed, there is still a closeness, almost of kinship, between a man and his work. How often have you heard the expression, "He is married to his job"? It might be a relationship of love or hate, of excitement or boredom, involvement or indifference. Here is Theodore Roethke's old florist:

OLD FLORIST

That hump of a man bunching chrysanthemums
Or pinching-back asters, or planting azaleas,
Tamping and stamping dirt into pots,—
How he could flick and pick
Rotten leaves or yellowy petals,
Or scoop out a weed close to flourishing roots,
Or make the dust buzz with a light spray,
Or drown a bug in one spit of tobacco juice,
Or fan life into wilted sweet-peas with his hat,
Or stand all night watering roses, his feet blue in
    rubber boots.

More than a list of what the job entails and some of the un-orthodox ways in which he does it, "a spit of tobacco juice," more than a description of the skill of the man, this is a poem about someone who understands and cares, in the deepest sense of the word, for flowers, who would, "stand all night watering roses, his feet blue in rubber boots."

This is how Michael Pacelli, a student, sees a particular photographer.

EXPOSED

He stays in the dark.
The brightness of daylight diffuses
his reality.
He mixes chemicals over paper
creates an image from nothing.
The moon and its faces are his obsession.
Crawling around at night, he finds

its good side.
Night after night he captures
the moon
from a sliver to its whole.
He seeks the perfect light
developing his dream.

and how Joe Dobrow sees his piano tuner

PIANO TUNER

He's comfortable in his plain blue jacket
his wide plain white tie.
The only thing fancy about him is his long
Italian name
and his long quick fingers.
His master ear at work
he tightens this string, loosens that
all the while enduring
the monotonous F sharps
which chase us into our quiet rooms.
The work finally done, he unlocks
his fingers, smiles a smile
wider than his tie
and the pop tunes of the 60's fill the house.
Then he stops playing, gets up
as if not wanting to leave
and takes off for the Johnson house
                              down the block.

and how Liz Weiss sees the Good Humor man

THE GOOD HUMOR MAN

He wouldn't be
himself
if he didn't have that
silver change spitter
around his waist
and a barrage
of bells
announcing his arrival.

Doctor, Lawyer, Indian Chief—write a poem about someone you know in terms of his or her job. Perhaps it's an exotic job in a circus or the routine work of a file clerk. You might begin by writing down all of the tasks or the skill that this job involves. This will give you a sense of how the person who does the job might feel. Consider the kind of clothes he/she wears. Do they make the man? Is he still the doctor when he takes off his white coat? Based upon the things that you see, what are the things that you can imagine? What is it that this person brings to the job—that center of himself that dictates his inner and outer clockwork? Don't tell us. Show us by the way he does his work.

After you've written your poem, you might want to read Ted Hughes' *Secretary*. What he sees of her life at the office leads to what he imagines her life is at home. Then take a look at Carol Muske's, *Swansong*, a recollection within a recollection of her dancing school teacher.

SECRETARY

If I should touch her she would shriek and weeping
Crawl off to nurse the terrible wound: all
Day like a starling under the bellies of bulls
She hurries among men, ducking, peeping,

Off in a whirl at the first move of a horn.
At dusk she scuttles down the gauntlet of lust
Like a clockwork mouse. Safe home at last
She mends socks with holes, shirts that are torn

For father and brother, and a delicate supper cooks
Goes to bed early, shuts out with the light
Her thirty years, and lies with buttocks tight,
Hiding her lovely eyes until day break.

SWANSONG
for Rose

The late Miss H. came to us Wednesdays at four
direct from the steno pool.
We waited, twenty of us in toe shoes,
slumped against her basement barre.

She was big,
her white hair bobbed,
her blue fox insurance against
ladies who called her déclassé.

Sometimes she told us how it was
when she danced *Les Sylphides* —
she, the ingénue with natural turnout,
withers drawn in the white light
of favored nations.
The Bolshoi sent its guns for her,
the heavy breathers from Minsk.
Miss H. leaped through their lines unruffled,
the season at her feet.
(Her lover Hans, a simple huntsman,
was at her side
the night in Dubrovnik
when a cab crushed her great toe.)

The swan died officially in St. Louis in '53
on a makeshift stage strewn with roses.
She gave her all,
then came to Minneapolis
where she taught us toe dance.

She often wept, sipping brandy,
nodding when the needle stuck
on a crack in *Romeo and Juliet*.
Those days we stood on ceremony:
mute sisters of the dance, we froze
holding second position till six
when the mothers came.

In the two poems that follow, *Cheap Jack and Cock-
eyed Miriam* and *At Every Gas Station There Are Mechanics*,
notice again where the speaker is in relation to his or her subject. In each poem, there is an imagined conversation between
the speaker and the subject; in *Mechanics*, an imagined drama
being played out. Because the speaker, the "I," also has a role,
as great if not greater than the subject's, we, too, are drawn in
more closely. We are offered more than what it takes to run a
fruit store or operate a garage. If a poem works, we become
the "I" who knows Cheap Jack or someone like him.

CHEAP JACK AND COCK-EYED MIRIAM

Cheap Jack and Cock-eyed Miriam,
this poem is for you,
owners of the fruit and
vegetable store on Avenue C,
street where my father died
on the Lower East Side of
Manhattan, U.S.A.

Cheap Jack, did the cheap mean that you
found it hard to part with a dollar
(in those days, of course, we said a penny)
or did it mean that you sold things cheap—
or did it mean both?
Is that how you made it maybe
from a pushcart to a stand
to a double front store
that became an institution
with your cock-eyed Miriam always at your side?

I can still see your sign in big letters:
CHEAP JACK AND COCK-EYED MIRIAM
(only I'm not sure about the hyphen which
I may be putting in from too much education).
I can't even remember what you looked like
(To tell the truth, my mother felt
your prices were too high for us)
but I imagine you, Jack,
born Jacob or Yankel
always with a wisecrack and
a ready smile on your lips
like Smilin' Jack in the comics.

And you, Miriam, were you actually wall-eyed,
like the kids I used to see waiting
in the Thirteenth St. Eye and Ear
with their poor eyes going in
all kinds of directions
and the little X marks
the doctors made over their eyebrows
as a symbol for "crossed,"
as a sign they had failed the test—
or were you just blind as a bat and
did they call you Four Eyes too?
But how sure of yourself you must have been

to let him make fun of you that way.
(How many men, after all, put their women
right beside them, even in a sign?)
I like to think of your great times
in the double bed together while
your eyeglasses watched from the night table.

Cheap Jack and Cock-eyed Miriam,
if you are still alive somewhere
(or if your children or grandchildren
are reading this in the family rooms
of their split-levels in the suburbs)
I want you to know that I love you
for you are a part of my childhood,
even more than the poems by men with 3 names
that are unforgettable
like John Greenleaf Whittier
or James Whitcomb Riley,
and even more than the poems by women with 3 names
that are forgettable
like Anna Mabel Hamilton
(or something like that).

And if you have made it together to
That Big Fruit Stand in the Sky—
(And how do you like your cheap boy
and cock-eyed girl, Mister Death?)—
I know that wherever you are
you are kidding around with the customers
and giving good value
and always full weight on the cherries.

                                        L. L. ZEIGER

AT EVERY GAS STATION THERE ARE MECHANICS

Around them my cleanliness stinks.
I smell it. And so do they.
I always want to tell them I used to box,
and change tires, and eat heroes.
It is my hands hanging out
of my sleeves like white gloves.
It is what I've not done, and do not know.
If they mention the differential
I pay whatever price. When
they tell me what's wrong beneath my hood
I nod, and become meek.

If they were to say I could not
have my car back, that it was theirs,
I would say thank you, you must be right.
And then I would walk home,
and create an accident.

STEPHEN DUNN

3

Sometimes we say of a person, he is a fox, and we can
conjure up all the fox-like things about him, like the shape of
his face, the color of his hair, the way he moves, that he's not
to be trusted. Or we wish for ourselves the freedom of a bird,
the grace and strength of a tiger. If, in your next life, you were
to be an animal and you had the power to chose, which animal
would you be? What is it about the life of that animal that at-
tracts you? Is there something in your life, today, something
about you, that could be translated? Would you want the pro-
tection and security of a Siamese cat? Do you picture yourself
cat-like in your movements? Is your hair tawny? your voice
deep? Are you used to having your way? Imagine your best
friend. Would he be a dolphin? a bear? Picture someone you
know as an inanimate object, a broom, for instance, or a chair.
What kind of chair? Picture someone as a car, a long black
sedan? a red sports car? Picture, as George MacBeth does, someone as a vegetable.

MARSHALL

It occurred to Marshall
that if he were a vegetable, he'd
be a bean. Not
one of your thin, stringy
green beans, or your

dry, marbly
Burlotti beans. No, he'd be
a broad bean,
a rich nutritious,
meaningful bean,

alert for advantages,
inquisitive with potatoes,
mixing with every kind
and condition of vegetable,
and a good friend

to meat and lager. Yes, he'd
leap from his huge
rough pod with a loud
popping sound
into the pot; always
in hot water
and out of it with a soft
heart inside
his horny carapace. He'd
carry the whole

world's hunger on
his broad shoulders, green
with best butter
or brown with gravy. And if
some starving Indian saw his

flesh bleeding
when the gas was turned on
or the knife went in
he'd accept the homage and prayers,
and become a god, and die like a man,

which, as things were, wasn't so easy.

This is another way of writing about people, another
way of making comparisons. Once George MacBeth has decided
that Marshall is a broad bean, he sets up all of the broad bean
qualities of both the man and the vegetable. Who do you know
who would qualify as a tomato?

The following poems are by students. Why has Tom
Richards written *Winter* in stanzas? How do the line breaks help
the poem to run down the page?

WINTER

If he were
a season
he'd be Winter.
Not one of these

winters which screams in
but a sly one that caught
you by
surprise, like the

clap of thunder that
comes just after
lightning has hit.
He'd be

the leader of
all seasons in
his own flawless way,
but not good for others.

With his blue icy tones, he'd
watch out for hot weather
standing up to it
from far away

but when it
got too close
he'd creep out
just as he'd come.

TOM RICHARDS

BIRD

He was a peacock
whose feathers were a shield
from the real world
that didn't care.

PETER GROSS

CANDY

She was a hollow chocolate
smooth and sweet on the outside
attracting people
        with her sugary veneer
but they never knew
that inside
there was no cherry.

ANDREA CHAIT

Run through your cast of characters. Write a poem
about someone you know or about yourself as an animal,
vegetable, or mineral. Try —

 a car—make, color, year, condition
 an element—earth, fire, air, water
 wind
 a flower—hothouse or wild
 a weed
 a time of day
 a musical instrument
 a tool
 an electrical appliance
 a color
 a candle
 an article of clothing

Begin by noting all of the similarities between the
person you're writing about and the thing he or she is being
compared to. How is her hair like parsley? his skin like a
canteloup? Consider attitudes and feelings as well as physical
characteristics. Marshall is a "meaningful bean." He "mixes
well." Again, you might do this in a very short poem in which
you use only one striking detail or you might do this using a
series of details. If you write about yourself as "I," you might
tell us what it's like to lead the kind of life you've chosen—a
stone in the bed of a river, the spoke of a wheel. What time do
you get up in the morning? What do you eat for snacks? Who's
your best friend? What about your life do you like most? What
would you change if you could?

   After you've written your poem, you might want to
look at *The Otter* and *A Cello as the Other Woman*. How do

poems like these and *Marshall* get started? Perhaps from some flash impression, a spark that crosses the arc and ignites, an image that the poet raises to language. But it's the illumination of both, the woman and the otter, and Seamus Heaney, on stage, sitting, "dry throated on the warm stones" that helps us to see. It's where *he* is and the authenticity of otter that locates *us* at the edge of the pool.

THE OTTER

When you plunged
The light of Tuscany wavered
And swung through the pool
From top to bottom.

I loved your wet head and smashing crawl,
Your fine swimmer's back and shoulders
Surfacing and surfacing again
This year and every year since.

I sat dry-throated on the warm stones.
You were beyond me.
The mellowed clarities, the grape-deep air
Thinned and disappointed.

Thank God for the slow loadening,
When I hold you now
We are close and deep
As the atmosphere on water.

My two hands are plumbed water
You are my palpable, lithe
Otter of memory
In the pool of the moment,

Turning to swim on your back,
Each silent, thigh-shaking kick
Re-tilting the light,
Heaving the cool at your neck.

And suddenly you're out,
Back again, intent as ever,
Heavy and frisky in your freshened pelt,
Printing the stones.

SEAMUS HEANEY

A CELLO AS THE OTHER WOMAN

She has a few scruples,
She didn't come to the wedding.
But after he carried me over the threshold
He went back and got her.

His friends called her "Gert."
Seeing her flat bosom and bulbous belly,
I thought she was a joke,
Stuck in her case in the corner.
At first when he took her out
His new wedding ring felt heavy.
He wanted to put it in his pocket.
I still didn't catch on.

When he said one night they'd be late
And he carried her home in his arms
Humming snatches of song,
Falling on the bed
Like some doped Argonaut;
When I saw his fingers pressing
The tendons along her neck
Till she whined ecstatically,
When she went along on our vacation,
I began to understand.

They've been together a long time now,
Longer than we have.
I sit with them as he oils her slick curves,
Waxes her horsehair bow,
Brings her strings to a true pitch,
And talks about her high lineage,
Her beauty, her antiquity.
Of course, they still go off
To some melodious reef
Where I can't get at them,
But I'm getting used to her.

As time passes I even find it comforting—
His preference for old ladies.
Sometimes, the morning after,
I find on his coat a long white hair.

JANE FLANDERS

Family photograph albums are another source for
finding people. Look through the old pictures of your parents
or your aunts and uncles. Study their faces, their clothes. Are
they posing or were they interrupted in the middle of something when the photo was taken? What are they saying? How
do you imagine their lives at that time? Look at a photo of
yourself. What were the circumstances that surround the picture? This is what Patricia Hampl writes about.

THE CAR IN THE PICTURE

My father is sitting on the grass
in a sleeveless cotton-ribbed undershirt.
He is looking off somewhere
to something we will never know about.
It must be night, it must be summer.
I am laughing. Chokecherry lips, tiny peg teeth.
My hand is touching his shoulder,
a daughter's doll hand,
hot ingot of joy impressing
itself into his life.
Behind us, that black car,
a case of beer on the running board,
a Chevy, "from before the war," as my father says.
From before me,
from the August nights when the men sat
together on the grass, watching
the green frill of the algae
lighten on the lake and become ghostly.
When someone would break
the silence to say,
You buy a Studebaker,
you buy a Rambler,
you'll *never* be sorry.

What we have here is more than a photograph. True, we can
picture the time of year, the time of day, the light on the lake,
the color of the car, what the father is wearing, but what we
also have is a memory, a feeling for that time and place in the
poet's life.

Susan Strayer Deal has more distance from her photo. She imagines a life, a little drama, for people she never knew.

DAGUERREOTYPE

Six boys all stamped
with their father's
face, lean on the wagon
and smile. They are
lanky, lean, in
overalls and no shirts.
The oldest and tallest
smiles conservatively,
holding spirit back.
The youngest boy grins
full force. They go up
and down the scale of smiling
from liberal to conservative.
The full bearded father
does not smile from his
seat on the wagon. He holds
the reins on horses the
photography cuts off. Looks
deep into my eyes and still
can't see me. A woman on
the porch of the farmhouse
watches her husband
and the boys posing
for the camera. Does not
look past them
who are just about
to ride off in the gray wagon
or go to the barn and out
of my hands, holding this picture
seventy years later.

Chose *your* photo. Walk into it. Look out of it. Write a poem that will make us see the photo and beyond the photo. Make the words more than the picture.

After you've written your poem, you might want to read the students' poems that follow. For each of them time is stopped and recorded. Life is suspended in the framework of the poem.

BOYS DRINKING FROM A PUMP

I bend my knees pitting my weight against
the weight of water.
My brother tilts his head waiting
for a taste.
He will never get one. Maybe then he did.
Now the water hangs, droplets, mid-air . . .
The grey leaves of the trees don't move
don't change.
I squint in the then yellow, now white light
       watching my brother.

COLIN SUMMERS

CLICK

Everything under this huge weeping willow tree
which blocks my grandmother's house
is green.
All you can see is the cool, shady porch.
The shadows testify that it is sunny.
It is springtime.
The dress my mother made me is green, too
little daisies all over, falling
in no particular pattern
and I am sporting it for the
first time, smiling broadly, obviously pleased
       with the day
        the green
        the house
and that it must be 3:30 and I am
up from my nap.

DEBORAH SKOLNIK

7

CLOTHES, ETC.

1

You have, perhaps, heard the expression, "You are what you eat." To a great extent, we are also what we wear. Some days are set aside for yellows and reds, and some days nothing will do but a black turtleneck. As there are nights for flamboyant bandannas, there are mornings for the blues. Gray is for the days we are cautious. Like the security blanket, we have our security clothes—an old sweater which might be too large or too small, but it does not itch and it has deep pockets (in which, if you're lucky, you'll find a few lifesavers). It's the sweater we grab for when we wonder, what. Some clothes we feel good in because we feel we look good—a shirt that's right for our eyes or our hair. Some clothes are too good to wear. We save them for a special occasion that, somehow, is never special enough. They're still waiting in the closet or the drawer. Not today. Then there are the clothes that have born witness— those that have seen us through the things we would like to remember or the things we would rather forget, not to mention the good luck clothes, like the tennis shirt that makes you a winner or the costume that transforms you from a Clark Kent. Finally, there are the clothes that someone has given you, a handmade gift or a hand-me-down that has stitched into the seams (for better or for worse) the giver. Pablo Neruda writes about a pair of socks that Maru Mori gave to him.

ODE TO MY SOCKS

Maru Mori brought me
a pair
of socks
which she knitted herself
with her sheepherder's hands,
two socks as soft
as rabbits.
I slipped my feet
into them
as though into
two
cases
knitted
with threads of
twilight
and goatskin.
Violent socks,
my feet were
two fish made
of wool,
two long sharks
sea-blue, shot
through
by one golden thread
two immense blackbirds,
two cannons:
my feet
were honored
in this way
by
these
heavenly socks.
They were
so handsome
for the first time
my feet seemed to me
unacceptable
like two decrepit
firemen, firemen
unworthy
of that woven
fire,

of those glowing
socks.

Nevertheless
I resisted
the sharp temptation
to save them somewhere
as schoolboys
keep fireflies,
as learned men
collect
sacred texts,
I resisted
the mad impulse
to put them
into a golden
cage
and each day give them
birdseed
and pieces of pink melon.
Like explorers
in the jungle who hand
over the very rare
green deer
to the spit
and eat it
with remorse,
I stretched out
my feet
and pulled on
the magnificent
socks
and then my shoes.

The moral
of my ode is this:
beauty is twice
beauty
and what is good is doubly
good
when it is a matter of two socks
made of wool
in winter.

PABLO NERUDA
(Translation by Robert Bly)

Singing the praises of these heavenly socks, Neruda compares them to fish, to blackbirds, to cannon, and to more. How many more can you find? He thinks to save them, "as learned men / collect / sacred texts." Through these extravagant comparisons, we know how priceless the socks are to him, and through these comparisons, we can better experience what they look like, how soft they are, and how warm.

Write a poem about something that you like to wear, or hate to wear, or never wear. You might include in your poem how you have come by the hat, sweater, scarf, or argyle socks. Was it a present? Handmade? Hand-me-down? Taken without permission while your sister was at college? Was it bought on sale? Does it fit? What does it look like that makes it special or ugly? How does it feel—as scratchy as what? How do you feel when you wear it? Try to include at least one comparison in your poem to help us to see more clearly what you see and how you feel. After you've written your poem, you might want to read about some of these things from the wardrobes of students.

ODE TO MY HANDKERCHIEF

given to me by
    and old
        friend
an embroidered "A"
    in the corner
then, clean and
    lily white
now yellow with age
    like the lady
        who gave it to me.

AMY BARASCH

CAMOUFLAGED GUARDIAN

This was me, my trademark
the camouflage jacket.
I brushed against the leaves
of a jungle
in every hallway.
I shot the enemy in every room
was captured
in every class.

I was bigger than life, a hero.
But what kind of hero can have
a jacket that's so small - -
certainly not
a real one.
So there it hangs
in my closet, guarding
my weaker clothes.

ANDY SCHARF

ODE TO MY JEANS

Nothing but a pair of jeans
nothing but slow fading denim
with bits of my life torn apart
patched by time, again and again.

Peter holds the left knee together.
A weekend in Boston covers the right.
Judy hangs from a thigh
reaching for James Dean running down the calf.

Nothing but the best summer in
my memory
painted in white and orange
splattered in red ink
held together by threads
of yellow and green.

DAVE PUMO

2

In the way that we form attachments to clothes, we form attachments to objects. The old teddy bear missing a nose still sits on the top shelf of the closet. The pillow, now spare and lumpy, still has its share of good dreams. The chair with threadbare arms is "just right." Even ordinary things, like an old car, a salt and pepper shaker, or a piece of string, can evoke a response or can be the subject of praise. These are some of the things students responded to.

THE SECRET KEEPER

Tangled and twisted
in the corner of a drawer
it came from something forgotten,
a present
long ago lost.
No color
dull yellow or hot pink
a coiled snake that never moves
it wrapped and
held something
something precious or
unwanted.
But it's gone.
It keeps its memories tied up
all knotted together.
I try to uncoil it
but it won't let out
its secrets.

AHN LEE

THE RED RIBBON

It is in a drawer all its own
carefully laid out, center stage
a piece of glowing satin
that makes me breathe deeply
and again I feel the hot sun and the wind
the power beneath me perfectly balanced
perfectly timed, moving like clockwork
how it feels like riding a wave all the way in.
Pride and glory fill me up,
but I close the drawer knowing
that winning isn't everything.

JILL HERZIG

ODE TO MY INDIAN FABRIC

It started with a square
warm red fabric
with squirming bright strings
like flying fish
jumping in and out
of shiny mirrored ponds.

I made it into a dress
exotic, untouched
but the scents of India lingered
until
it shrank or maybe I grew.

Too good to waste
I made it into a pillow
that acts as a mirror
a reflection of my life.

LISA PODOS

ODE TO A DRAWING PAD

With good posture
standing
tall in the back of
my closet is
Grumbacher 300.
Never tainted
by paint
it stands cool white and silken.
Never a page
ripped out in frustration.
Maybe never to
know purple and yellow
my Grumbacher 300
knows the black
of my closet.

NAOMI YANG

Write a poem that is a response to

a baseball mitt	a mirror
a pillow	shoelaces
braces	an address book
eye glasses	a bathtub
a desk blotter	a rocking chair

or any object you have some feelings about. Whether it be a
praise or a lament, you might begin by addressing the object
directly. "Oh, braces, you, in whose reflection . . ." What might
they be praised or blamed for? Consider, for example, the sad-
ness of shoelaces or the secrecy of the blotter. What questions

would you like to ask the bathtub? Does it have a favorite song? a favorite soap? How does it consider its predicament? How do you?

3

Although for the most part we take them for granted, the things to which we are unquestionably attached are the parts of our body. David Young pays tribute to his wrists.

POEM FOR WRISTS

Wrists! I want to
write you a poem you
whom nurses finger watches
circle razors open
handcuffs chill—you are
taken for granted wrists!
therefore assert yourselves
take charge of your
unruly friends the hands
keep them from triggers, off
necks give them a light
touch have them wave bye-bye
teach them to let
go at the right moment oh
wrists shy angles of the arm
on whom farms flyrods
shovels whips and poems
so naturally depend.

Write a poem for a part of your body. Consider all of the functions, for example, of your nose, not to mention the myriad things it smells. What instructions would you give it? What precautions would you tell it to take? How would you suggest it consider itself in the light of other noses, a chef's nose or an undertaker's nose or the nose of your neighbor. What can a nose be compared to?

In deciding which part of the body to write to, you might consider

the liver	the tonsils
the lungs	the adenoids
the tongue	the ear lobes
the fingernails	the soles of your feet
the appendix	shoulders

You might begin with an inventory of all of the functions, say of fingernails. Which functions are worthy of praise? Which deserve blame? What suggestions do you have for improvement? What should they be wary of? Talk to them directly, "Fingernails!" What promises can you make them? Dare to say something outlandish.

4

Imagine for a moment
the still life of our meals
meat followed by yellow cheese
grapes pale against the blue armor of fish.

from The Invention of Cuisine
by CAROL MUSKE

Before tables were set with silver and crystal, before meals were arranged by color, before the preparation of food came to be known as cuisine, imagine how even a primitive man must have had his particular fondness for a delicacy like snake or speckled trout. As we have our favorite clothes and favorite objects, we have our favorite foods. No accounting why the world is divided into chocolate lovers and vanilla lovers, only that they exist. Beyond nourishment, food has its own kind of pleasure, something to do with the way it looks and the way it feels; of course, the way it tastes. Nuts crunch, champagne bubbles on the roof of your mouth, tapioca slides.

Set a bowl of fruit before you, or a bunch of vegetables, and take another look at what you may have always taken for granted. Run your thumb over the skin of an orange. Dismantle its sections. Peel an onion, layer by layer. Slice it open and find its two eyes. Stringbeans have fur; carrots, mustaches. Split a pear and examine its core. What can an artichoke be compared to? What is the implied comparison when Charles Simic says,

"Aunt Lettuce, I want to look under your skirt." How is a watermelon like a Buddha?

WATERMELONS

Green Buddhas
On the fruit stand.
We eat the smile
And spit out the teeth.

CHARLES SIMIC

Write a poem about a food you cannot live without. It might be an exotic food like chocolate covered violets or something everyday, like spaghetti. Consider its color, tecture, taste, smell—which foods it goes well with, when you like to eat it, what it can be compared to. Make us lick our lips.

After you have written your poem, you might want to read what Pablo Neruda has written about a tomato and what John Baird and Ava Fradkin, students, have written about garlic and strawberries. A good way to finish the meal might be with Donald Hall's *O Cheese*.

If you still have not had your fill of poems, at the end of the chapter are other poems that have to do with clothes, etc.

ODE TO THE TOMATO

The street
drowns in tomatoes:
noon,
summer,
light
breaks
in two
tomato
halves,
and the streets
run
with juice.
In December
the tomato
cuts loose,
invades
kitchens,
takes over lunches,

settles
at rest
on sideboards,
with the glasses,
butter dishes
blue salt-cellars.
It has
its own radiance,
a goodly majesty.
Too bad we must
assassinate:
a knife
plunges
into its living pulp,
red
viscera,
a fresh,
deep,
inexhaustible
sun
floods the salads
of Chile,
beds cheerfully
with the blonde onion,
and to celebrate
oil
the filial essence
of the olive tree
lets itself fall
over its gaping hemispheres,
the pimento
adds
its fragrance,
salt its magnetism—
we have the day's
wedding:
parsley
flaunts
its little flags,
potatoes
thump to a boil,
the roasts
beat
down the door

with their aromas:
it's time!
let's go!
and upon
the table,
belted by summer,
tomatoes,
stars of the earth
stars multiplied
and fertile
show off
their convolutions,
canals
and plenitudes
and the abundance
boneless,
without husk
or scale or thorn,
grant us
the festival
of ardent colour
and all-embracing freshness.

PABLO NERUDA·
(Translation by Nathaniel Tarn)

GARLIC

Red lights flashing
Fire trucks rushing
Danger
It comes again
Tastebuds scream
Body quivers
Oh linger on, burning Italian dream!

JOHN BAIRD

STRAWBERRIES

I walked on thousands of strawberries
and they squished up through my toes
I rolled in strawberries
and they covered me with red
I drank sweet smelling juice
and licked my lips
I molded strawberry sculptures
and watched them melt
I washed my hair with strawberries
and lay
on a carpet of green stems
to dry

AVA FRADKIN

O CHEESE

In the pantry the dear dense cheeses, Cheddars and harsh
Lancashires; Gorgonzola with its magnanimous manner;
the clipped speech of Roquefort; and a head of Stilton
that speaks in a sensuous riddling tongue like Druids.

O cheeses of gravity, cheeses of wistfulness, cheeses
that weep continually because they know they will die.
O cheeses of victory, cheeses wise in defeat, cheeses
fat as a cushion, lolling in bed until noon.

Liederkranz ebullient, jumping like a small dog, noisy;
Pont l'Evéque intellectual, and quite well informed;
    Emmentaler
decent and loyal, a little deaf in the right ear;
and Brie the revealing experience, instantaneous and pro-
    found.

O cheeses that dance in the moonlight, cheeses
that mingle with sausages, cheeses of Stonehenge.
O cheeses that are shy, that linger in the doorway,
eyes looking down, cheeses spectacular as fireworks.

Reblochon openly sexual; Caerphilly like pine trees, small
at the timberline; Port du Salut in love; Caprice des Dieux
eloquent, tactful, like a thousand-year-old hostess;
and Dolcelatte, always generous to a fault.

O village of cheeses, I make you this poem of cheeses,
O family of cheeses, living together in pantries,
O cheeses that keep to your own nature, like a lucky
   couple,
this solitude, this energy, these bodies slowly dying.

DONALD HALL

THE MITTENS MY GRANDMOTHER MADE

My grandmother made me some mittens
knowing I like them better than gloves
knowing I like the way all four fingers
keep each other warm, the way
they can huddle together into a fist
and the isolated thumb
abandoning his own sweater
to join the rest of the crowd.

And as I wear these mittens
I think of my grandmother,
her hands working like cricket legs all night
and the rocking chair thumping like a dog's tail,
and I think of my grandmother, thinking of me
trudging through the winter,
bundled up like a bear,
my feet buried in eskimo boots
and my hands in her mittens.

LAURA GILPIN

GYM SHORTS

You really look good in those gym shorts
now that they're worn
and you're filled out to fit them
so manly.
You used to look good way back then, too
Was it ten years ago?
That long?

Yes. I saw the games. I was watching.
Watching those gym shorts
grip muscled sides
as you dribbled and sped
playing king of the court.
Watched how the gold stripe you alone wore
marked you apart

from the bodies rising
when you netted the ball
as if picking a rose.
How your shorts sort of fluttered
against trembling thighs
when you sprang to the floor
and ceiling spotlights stroked you.

You were sweat and smiles and modest lies
leaning on the railing
at halftime.
You shivered. So I loaned you my coat.
You thanked me.
Those gym shorts were new then,
shining blue
like children's wishes.

FELICE PICANO

HERE ARE MY BLACK CLOTHES

I think now it is better to love no one
than to love you. Here are my black clothes,
and tired nightgowns and robes fraying
in many places. Why should they hang useless
as though I were going naked? You liked me well enough
in black; I will make you a gift of these objects.
You will want to touch them with your mouth, run
your fingers through the thin
tender underthings and I
will not need them in my new life.

LOUISE GLÜCK

BESTIARY FOR THE FINGERS OF MY RIGHT HAND

1

Thumb, loose tooth of a horse.
Rooster to his hens.
Horn of a devil. Fat worm
They have attached to my flesh
At the time of my birth.
It takes four to hold him down,
Bend him in half, until the bone
Begins to whimper.

Cut him off. He can take care
Of himself. Take root in the earth,
Or go hunting with wolves.

2

The second points the way.
True way. The path crosses the earth,
The moon and some stars.
Watch he points further.
He points to himself.

3

The middle one has backache.
Stiff, still unaccustomed to this life;
An old man at birth. It's about something
That he had lost,
That he looks for within my hand,
The way a dog looks
For fleas
With a sharp tooth.

4

The fourth is mystery.
Sometimes as my hand
Rests on the table
He jumps by himself
As though someone called his name.

After each bone, finger,
I come to him, troubled.

5

Something stirs in the fifth
Something perpetually at the point
Of birth. Weak and submissive,
His touch is gentle.
It weighs a tear.
It takes the mote out of the eye.

CHARLES SIMIC

homage to my hair

when i feel her jump up and dance
i hear the music! my God
i'm talking about my nappy hair!
she's a challenge to your hand
Black man
she is as tasty on your tongue as good greens
Black man,
she can touch your mind
with her electric fingers and
the grayer she do get, good God,
the Blacker she do be!

LUCILLE CLIFTON

8

SOUND/SILENCE

1

Like music, poetry is meant to be heard. What sets it apart from other kinds of writing is its music—the sound of the words in concert with other words, the way the syntax can sing. And like the composer, the poet has a whole keyboard at his disposal. For starters, there are the twenty-six letters of the alphabet and all their combinations and variations, not to mention rhythm and rhyme and the white spaces in between.

Sound, for the poet, makes sense in both senses of the word. The harsh sounds and the soft sounds, like the high notes and the low notes, contribute to the overall effect and help us to hear and understand the experience of the poem. Read *November Night* aloud and listen.

NOVEMBER NIGHT

Listen . . .
With faint dry sound,
Like steps of passing ghosts
The leaves, frost-crisped, break from the trees
And fall.

ADELAIDE CRAPSEY

After the word, "Listen," the poet gives us three dots to get ready. Which words help you to hear someone walking through

114

dead leaves? Take another look at the length of the lines, how they swell and diminish, how "And fall" does double duty. If you were to count the syllables in each they would be 2 4 6 8 2, the form of a *cinquain*. How does this opening and closing of the line add to the experience of the poem? Which words help us to hear the song of the cricket in Carl Sandburg's poem?

SPLINTER

The voice of the last cricket
across the first frost
is one kind of good-by.
It is so thin a splinter of singing.

But in order to find out about any of this, you must put on your ears. One of the ways to begin is to listen to what goes on inside your head while you're chewing. Start with a stalk of celery. Chew—mouth open, mouth closed, quickly, slowly. Write down all of the words that sound like the sound you're making as you chew. When you run out of words that you know, make up words that will translate what you hear. You'll probably come up with words like munch and crunch and crack. Listen to yourself and let them spin out.

Keep chewing, and as you chew write down all of the things that the sound reminds you of—things that have nothing to do with celery. What do you hear? What do your eyes see? footsteps on the frozen snow? a tree splintering?

Try a marshmallow. Again write down all of the words that you hear as you chew. You'll probably come up with words like whoosh and slosh, words with long vowels and the soft "sh" sound. The word marshmallow, itself, with its long vowels and its mmmmm's, lllll's, and sh, sounds like what it is. What are your associations with those squishes? What do you hear in your mind's eye?

Write a poem from a sound. It might be an inventory of all the things you think of in connection with a sigh, or it might be one particular thing triggered by a whisper. Let the sound be the connection. You may be surprised where it will take you, how it will connect things you would never imagine had any connection. This is one of the ways our minds make comparisons, perhaps the way Carl Sandburg got to cricket and splinter.

The following are possibilities:

a buzz	sloshing
a whine	cracking
a thud	sizzling
whispers	tapping
sighs	sniffing
a roar	a rumble

Rachel Miller, a student, started with sssss

SSSSSSS

SSSSSS
steam
steam heat
says I used to dance
in classrooms
where big windows
kept out
the beckoning
snow fresh air.
Steam whisped hot strokes
on our faces
and mirrors
would steam-fog and distort
and shorten
our tall thin bodies.
We danced
adagio
slow in winter
when the ssssss
steam heat was
hotter than the summer sun.

Experience comes to us in its own phrases, its own rhythm, and its own sounds. Rachel's associations with ssssss steam is dancing, and the poem creates its own kind of dance rhythm. What also contributes to its music is the repetition that opens and closes the poem and the slant rhyme (dance/classrooms, distort/shorten) in between.

2

A good place to listen to sound effects is a sporting event. Aside from the cheers and boos and someone yelling, "Hot dogs and cold soda," what are the sounds of a basketball game? How do they differ from those of a tennis match? As each game has its unique sounds and its unique rules, each has its own vocabulary. And sometimes, even the words of a game, like stick and puck, ice and glide, can help us to hear it in writing. May Swenson does an

ANALYSIS OF BASEBALL

It's about
the ball,
the bat,
and the mitt.
Ball hits
bat, or it
hits mitt.
Bat doesn't
hit ball. Bat
meets it.
Ball bounces
off bat, flies
air, or thuds
ground (dud)
or it
fits mitt.

Bat waits
for ball
to mate.
Ball hates
to take bat's
bait. Ball
flirts, bat's
late, don't
keep the date.
Ball goes in
(thwack) to mitt,
and goes out
(thwack) back
to mitt.

Ball fits
mitt, but
not all
the time.
Sometimes
ball gets hit
(pow) when bat
meets it,
and sails
to a place
where mitt
has to quit
in disgrace.
That's about
the bases
loaded
about 40,000
fans exploded.

It's about
the ball,
the bat,
the mitt,
the bases
and the fans.
It's done
on a diamond,
and for fun.
It's about
home, and it's
about run.

You've probably noticed the length (or shortness) of the
lines and the words and how many of the words end in "t." This
is one of the ways sound works hand in glove with meaning.
You've probably also noticed the words that imitate the sound—
like thwack and thud. When a word imitates what it sounds like,
we call it *onomatopoetic*, which comes from the Greek—to make
a name. So dud and pow have made names for themselves. How
do the line breaks and the repetition imitate the pace of the
game?

Damon Krukowski, a student, gives us his version of

POKER

The snap of the cards
The click of the chips
The crunch of the pretzel
The swish of the beer

The whoop of the winner
The groan of the other
The sweep of the table
The clack of the stack

Here is what sound can do because of meaning. Here is what
sound can do because of placement. The sounds of the words,
snap, click, crunch, and the repetition of the syntax give us a
sense of the way the game is played—the finality of the clack
of the stack.

Write a poem that will make us feel that we are the
spectators at a game. It might be a game like basketball or
hockey. It might be a street game like tag, or a quiet game like
chess. What we want is a ringside seat.

3

Now tune in to the whole world—all of its noises—
morning sounds, night sounds, the throat clearing and page
turning in a library, the cup returned to its saucer, the specifics
of thunder. Listen to what William Carlos Williams has to say in

THE POEM

It's all in
the sound. A song.
Seldom a song. It should

be a song—made of
particulars, wasps,
a gentian—something
immediate, open

scissors, a lady's
eyes—waking
centrifugal, centripetal.

Listen for the song that is "seldom a song," the "song made of particulars." "It's all," he says, "in the sound." Listen to these poems by students.

MIDNIGHT ATTIC

and the crack
of the mousetrap as it
snapped down
on the empty wood
to mark
a little victory

ANDY SCHARF

WINTER MORNINGS

I remember icy December mornings,
I would go down to the lake.
Frozen soil iced by the morning dew
crunched under my boots.
I would sit on the bench for a while
listening to the forest
a sparrow whistling its waking song
a rabbit through the heavy brush.
The lake was newly frozen.
I could hear it crackle under my blades
protesting my intrusion.

STEVE ABRAMS

The internal rhyme of the vowels in *Midnight Attic*, little and victory, crack, mousetrap, and snapped, is one kind of music. Which words make the music in *Winter Mornings*? Sounds and syllables seem to discover each other. Perhaps this is how William Carlos Williams came to "centrifugal, centripetal."

Write a poem about something noisy. Stay with what you hear, with what you feel, and a pattern of sound will emerge. We each have our own private words, words we like the sound of. Go with those words. They are yours, and they will lead you to what you want to say. You might begin with the line, "You're not listening . . ." or just keep it in mind as you write. Make us hear what you hear.

After you've written your poem, you might want to read another of May Swenson's.

THE WATCH

When I
took my
watch to the watchfixer I
felt privileged but also pained to watch the operation. He
had long fingernails and a voluntary squint. He
fixed a magnifying cup over his
squint eye. He
undressed my
watch. I
watched him
split
her into three layers and lay her
middle (a quivering viscera) in a circle on a little plinth. He
shoved shirtsleeves up, and leaned like an ogre over my
naked watch, and with critical pincers poked and stirred. He
lifted out little private things with a magnet too tiny for me
to watch, almost. "Watch out!" I
almost said. His
eye watched, enlarged, the secrets of my
watch, and I
watched anxiously. Because what if he
touched her
ticker too rough, and she
gave up the ghost out of pure fright? Or put her
things back backwards so she'd
run backwards after this? Or he
might lose a minuscule part, connected to her
exquisite heart, and mix her
up, instead of fix her.
And all the time
pieces on the walls, on the shelves told the time,
told the time
in swishes and ticks,
and seemed to be gloating as they watched and told. I
felt faint. I
was about to lose my
breath (my
ticker going lickety-split) when watchfixer clipped her
three slices together with a gleam and two flicks of his
tools like chopsticks. He
spat out his
eye, and lifted her
high, gave her

a twist, set her
hands right, and laid her
little face, quite as usual, in its place on my
wrist.

How is the watch more than a watch? Which words make it
tick?

4

If one side of the coin is sound, the other is silence.
Things that are silent, because of their very silence, can elo-
quently set off loud emotional reverberations. The poet,
Marianne Moore, wrote, "The deepest feeling always shows
itself in silence." In this translation of Ryota by Kenneth
Rexroth, three quiet lines become a dramatic situation.

No one spoke
the host, the guests
the white chrysanthemums.

What do you imagine preceded the silence? What might follow? Why is white the perfect color for the chrysanthemums?
    In the way that a painting is noisy or still through the
selection of its details, through its colors and its light, so, too,
a poem can be noisy or still. Each of the following poems
paints a still life—still in the sense of movement, still in the
sense of sound. Which particular details compose the quiet?
Against the backdrop of these silences, what do the poets
hear? What do you hear?

NANTUCKET

Flowers through the window
lavender and yellow

changed by white curtains—
Smell of cleanliness—

Sunshine of late afternoon—
On the glass tray

a glass pitcher, the tumbler
turned down, by which

a key is lying—And the
immaculate white bed

WILLIAM CARLOS WILLIAMS

A SUMMER NIGHT

At the end of the street
a porch light is burning,
showing the way. How simple,
how perfect it seems: the darkness,
the white house like a passage
through summer and into
a snowfield. Night after night,
the lamp comes on at dusk,
the end of the street
stands open and white,
and an old woman sits there
tending the lonely gate.

TED KOOSER

LISTENING IN OCTOBER

In the quiet house
a lamp is burning
where the book of autumn
lies open on a table.

There is tea with milk
in heavy mugs,
brown raisin cake, and thoughts
that stir the heart
with promises of death.

We sit without words,
gazing past the limit
of fire, into the towering
darkness . . .

There are silences so deep
you can hear
the journeys of the soul,
enormous footsteps
downward in a freezing earth.

JOHN HAINES

Motions, gestures, facial expressions, all of them silent, can make us hear more clearly than words. Like a silent film, Laura Gilpin's poem speaks through its motions and its gestures; Marge Piercy's through the expression in the eyes of the hare.

HARE IN WINTER

The wounded hare looks out
of the trap at me.
Animals rarely
force us
to meet their gaze.
How food stares.
Suddenly my tongue
floats in blood.

MARGE PIERCY

SPRING

for Aunt Aggie

Very early every morning
my great aunt, still in her
bathrobe and bedroom slippers,
goes out into the yard
to see the flowers.

Slowly, taking great care
with each step, she walks first
to the row of azaleas by the fence
stopping for a long time
at each one,

then to the camellias
which are almost gone
where she brushes away
the dead flowers, then
to the dogwood where

she pulls away several strands
of Spanish moss, then
to the wisteria where she
leans down to smell them,
then to the pear tree,

then to the lily bed,
to the hydrangeas, to
the magnolia fuscata
where the petals fall
loosely into her hand.

And then she stops and
looking back over all of them
she nods. Finally she turns
and begins the long walk
back towards the house.

And when she sits quietly
in the rocking chair by the window,
the hem of her bathrobe
is still wet with dew.

LAURA GILPIN

Think of the things you know that are absolutely
silent—mushrooms, a chair, rage, an icicle, smoke, a candle, a
wink, someone waving goodbye. Which places are silent—cellars,
closets, the insides of pockets or of stones? What are the sounds
of silence in *your* lonely room? These are some poems by
students.

INTRUDER

I hang out my window
cold night
slinking in
like a silent intruder
invading my privacy
and my warm room
cold night air
silent intruder
creep in
as you like
invade
as you like
for I am lonely

JULIA ROSENBLUM

VISIT

You don't want to be here—
I can tell—but you
won't say so—
an almost movement held
completely still.

HANNAH HIGGINS

READING

A low nasty day
perfectly still
my eyes begin to slip
through the holes between the words
in the alleys running
from line to line.
It has been on my mind a week now.
I am afraid to tell.

ROBIN BIERMAN

RERUN

I lie in bed watching
the insides
of my eyelids
on which the whole day
is told in story form
but I never
hear a word.

JESSICA NAROWLANSKY

Write a quiet poem. Watch someone doing something quiet. Listen to what has not been said out loud. Put yourself in a place that is quiet. What do you overhear in yourself? Look at something quiet. What is it telling you? In its own words, let us in on its secret.

Then, you might want to look at William Stafford's *Vacation Trip*, Norman MacCaig's *Balances*, and Alden Nowlan's *Waiting for Her*. Each of these plays off sound against the silence or silence against the sound.

VACATION TRIP

The loudest sound in our car
was Mother being glum;

> the little chiding valves
> a surge of detergent oil,
> all that deep chaos,
> the relentless accurate fire,
> the drive shaft wild to arrive,

and, tugging along behind in its great
big balloon,
that looming piece of her mind—

"I wish I hadn't come."

WILLIAM STAFFORD

BALANCES

I like almost imperceptibles, near still lifes—
a limpet sloping full-tilt down a rock:
thunder mooching among the mountains, trailing
delicate diminuendos: a mushroom
hoisting a paving slab on its darning-egg head:

the brooch on her dress
rising so quietly, so quietly falling.

Don't judge me by that: I like suddennesses too—
fistfuls, platefuls, ewers of snow slithered
from a larch tree: the far away Chinese music
of gorse pods popping: a tower bell stunning
the black air of a black night with one dazing blow:

And a key turning in the door of a quiet house
when I didn't know she was coming.

NORMAN MacCAIG

WAITING FOR HER

Waiting for her,
rain on the windshield,
cars passing
their tires hissing
on the black pavement;

one minute the rain
pounding the car roof
as drummers
must have pounded
their drums at old executions,
with their fists
not wanting to hear the screams;

the next minute so quiet
I can hear my cigarette
burning when I inhale.

I listen
for her, I know how
she walks at night
and in the rain, with a different rhythm.

I brace myself to pretend
if she comes I was sure she'd come,
if she doesn't that I don't care.

ALDEN NOWLAN

9
PERSONA

As very young children, we begin to try on other people to help us understand who we really are and how the world works. As if they were our own, we go through the motions of other lives. We become not only the good guy who gallops off into the sunset and the bad guy who falls dead in the games we invent but, even earlier, we become those imaginary people who inhabit the forests and the gingerbread houses in fairy tales. These are the roles we would slip into, unaware, when we read or were read to. This is the enchantment of fairy tales for the very young—this granting of unlimited power to win out over wicked queens and ugly sisters, to kill the giant, to be kissed awake by a handsome prince; indeed, to spin flax into gold. This is how, against almost overwhelming odds, we could fight all the real battles of childhood and how, in the end, live happily ever after.

Older now, and in some ways wiser, let's try to invent the story after the story, or the story behind the story. Saved from the witch, home safe with their father, what would Gretel say years later? This is the territory Louise Glück explores in

GRETEL IN DARKNESS

This is the world we wanted.
All who would have seen us dead
are dead. I hear the witch's cry
break in the moonlight through a sheet
of sugar: God rewards.
Her tongue shrivels into gas

Now, far from women's arms
and memory of women, in our father's hut
we sleep, are never hungry.
Why do I not forget?
My father bars the door, bars harm
from this house, and it is years.

No one remembers. Even you, my brother,
summer afternoons you look at me as though
you meant to leave,
as though it never happened.
But I killed for you. I see armed firs,
the spires of that gleaming kiln—

Nights I turn to you to hold me
but you are not there.
Am I alone? Spies
hiss in the stillness, Hansel,
we are there still and it is real, real,
that black forest and the fire in earnest.

Louise Glück has *become* Gretel. This is what we call
assuming a persona—the writer speaking in the voice of someone else, the writer wearing a mask. Louise Glück has imagined
another ending and, in the voice of Gretel, she tells us something about her life afterward. We see Hansel and their father
through her eyes but, mostly, we see Gretel. We know how she
feels. We can detect the loneliness and disappointment in her
voice. Talking to Hansel she says,

You look at me as though
you meant to leave
as though it never happened. . . .

What do you think Hansel might answer?

Billy Frischling, a student, tongue in cheek, has assumed the persona of

SNOW WHITE'S PRINCE

Oh, woe is me.
Why did I ever choose
that route through the forest?
Hundreds of ways but I had to choose
the route that destined me
to a life with Snow White.
Everyone thinks we lived happily
ever after,
a handsome young prince and a beautiful maiden,
a match made in heaven.
I wish the world knew the true story.
Nobody ever told me
about Snow White's large family
which visits, constantly.
Nobody told me how attached she was
to the seven dwarfs
that they would move in with us.
Nobody told me that the witch had a sister
who would seek revenge.
I am beginning to think that with my kiss
that gave Snow White life
I ended mine.

Michelle Saks has written in a more serious voice what Snow White might have answered.

SNOW WHITE

So you gave me the kiss of life
made me wake from my fairied sleep.
A hundred years I was peaceful
in fantasy.
Why did you waken me to your world?
You never knew I pricked my finger
to voyage to the happily ever after.
Uprooted, I am imprisoned
in life, my fairy prince.
You have sentenced me.

Although both of these poems have to do with the same story and the same disillusionment "ever after," each of the writers has taken on a different *tone*. Which details and which language help us to distinguish that difference? What is the tone of the following poem by Debi Brenin, a student?

AND

happily ever after
did not last forever.
From rags to riches
did not happen
so easily.
I do not fit in here
with the kings and queens
of never never land.
My dreams of glass slippers
shattered to a million pieces
I will say good-bye to all of this
and start another
once upon a time.

Beginning with the details of the stories as we know them, each of the poems moves on to another place, other characters, a surprising motivation. Each of the poems is a kind of drama. The poem that follows catches us at the climax of the story. By imagining what he would think (we all know what's going to happen), Lisa Freedman fleshes out the character of the Big Bad Wolf.

THE BIG BAD WOLF

Rather an inconvenience, really, for I'd
like to
Relish my food slowly
Crunch each bone fondly.
But there are advantages to a three course meal
The total pleasure of
Greasy, salty gluttony
Yet, I must remain calm.
I don't want to become short of
Breath
At the thought.
Besides, it's not dignified.

I have a reputation
To keep up.
Triumphing over the last house
Will truly immortalize me.
I dream of a statue in my figure
Noble profile
My glistening nose and whiskers clipped
So handsome.
The strongest lungs in the world
They'll say.

Pick a fairy tale you have always liked. You may have
to go back to Grimm or Andersen to get all the facts. You'll
probably be surprised at the scant characterization. People are
either kind or evil, clever or stupid, victims or victimizers, and
they are, by and large, described according to size and looks
and strength. This gives you plenty of leeway to introduce
those feelings that characterize real people. Write a poem in the
voice of one of the characters and tell his or her side of the story.
You might tell the sequel and use as an opening line, "Now that
it is ever after, we are not so happy . . ." or set the story straight,
"That was not the way it happened . . ." or become the Monday
morning quarterback, "If only I had not touched the spinning
wheel . . ." Some fairy tales end with, "If they have not died,
they live there still." You might consider

Goldilocks living with the three bears
Cinderella's foot growing too big for the slipper
Jack becoming a banker
The third little pig cornering the market on bricks

or in a more serious vein

Rapunzel's response to the parents who sacrificed her
The queen's regrets over Rumpelstiltskin
Hansel's reply to Louise Glück's Gretel
Red Riding Hood's devotion to the woodsman

If you are the princess who slept on the pea, let us know
the color of the quilt, how the light came through the window.
Ground us in the facts we know, but reveal a life according to
your lights.
After you have written your poem, you might want to
take a look at *Jack, Afterwards* and *From the Journals of the*

Frog Prince. Talking to someone, to you, the reader, Jack is trying to figure out how it all happened, ". . . what it all meant." "Why, me?" In reconstructing the story, he mulls over the particulars, the giant, the beanstalk, the cow, the old man. The journal of the frog prince is full of its own kind of particulars, the intimate details of his life together with the princess. That it is a journal entry allows the prince to make these kinds of revelations. In both cases, or in any case, the fairy tale can only come true for the reader if we have the facts, the very particulars that gave the fairy tale its reality in the first place.

JACK, AFTERWARDS

It's difficult to say what it all meant.
The whole experience, in memory,
Seems like a story someone might invent
Who was both mad and congenitally cheery.
I have to remind myself, it happened to me.
The stalk's gone now, and Alma, the old cow;
And I fear only the dream with the shadow.

My mother had a lot to do with it.
In fact, you might say it was her beanstalk—
She scattered the seeds, I didn't, when she hit
My full hand and said all I was good for was talk.
She haunted me in those days: I couldn't walk
Anywhere without seeing her face,
Even on the crone in the giant's palace.

Throughout this whole time, my father was dead.
I think I must have felt his not-being-there
More than I would have his being-there. Instead
Of his snoring, his absence was everywhere.
So the old man with the beans, poor and threadbare
As he was, became the more important
To my boyish needs, Not to mention the giant.

Oddly enough, the beanstalk itself, which some
Might think the most wonderful part of all this,
Pales in time's perspective. Though my true home
Between the earth and sky, and though no less
Than magic, that stalk, in the last analysis,
Was but a means to an end. Yet, I must say,
I still recall the beanflowers' sweet bouquet.

Then there's the giant. What can be said? Nothing
And everything. Or this: if the truth be known
About someone so great, it was surprising
How vulnerable he seemed, and how alone.
Not that I wasn't frightened. I was, to the bone—
But it was his weakness, joined to such power,
I feared most, and fear now, any late hour.

The fruits of it all were gold, a hen, and a harp.
I wish I could say I miss my poverty,
When my appetite, if not my wit, was sharp,
But I don't. A little fat hasn't hurt me
Much. Still it's that strange harp's melody,
Beauty willing itself, not golden eggs,
Whose loss would leave me, I hope, one who begs.

Of everything, the strangest was to see
Alma the cow come back home at the end,
Her two horns wreathed in wild briony
And traveler's joy. Did the old man send
Her as a gift? She seemed, somehow, lightened.
I'd like to think I traded her away
To get her back, sea-changed, in such array.

So I sit here, my dying, blind mother
To tend to, and wonder how it was
I escaped, smiling, from such an adventure.
If events in those days conformed to laws,
I'd like to know—not least, nor only, because
What happened then still makes me ask, Why me?
Not even my mother knew, when she could see.

PHILIP DACEY

FROM THE JOURNALS OF THE FROG PRINCE

In March I dreamed of mud,
sheets of mud over the ballroom chairs and table,
rainbow slicks of mud under the throne.
In April I saw mud of clouds and mud of sun.
Now in May I find excuses to linger in the kitchen
for wafts of silt and ale,
cinnamon and river bottom,
tender scallion and sour underlog.

At night I cannot sleep.
I am listening for the dribble of mud
climbing the stairs to our bedroom
as if a child in a wet bathing suit ran
up them in the dark.

Last night I said, "Face it, you're bored
How many times can you live over
with the same excitement
that moment when the princess leans
into the well, her face a petal
falling to the surface of the water
as you rise like a bubble to her lips,
the golden ball bursting from your mouth?"
Remember how she hurled you against the wall,
your body cracking open,
skin shrivelling to the bone,
the green pod of your heart splitting in two,
and her face imprinted with every moment
of your transformation?

I no longer tremble.

Night after night I lie beside her.
"Why is your forehead so cool and damp?" she asks.
Her breasts are soft and dry as flour.
The hand that brushes my head is feverish.
At her touch I long for wet leaves,
the slap of water against rocks.

"What are you thinking of?" she asks.
How can I tell her
I am thinking of the green skin
shoved like wet pants behind the Directoire desk?
Or tell her I am mortgaged to the hilt
of my sword, to the leek-green tip of my soul?
Someday I will drag her by her hair
to the river—and what? Drown her?
Show her the green flame of my self rising at her feet?
But there's no more violence in her
than in a fence or a gate.

"What are you thinking of?" she whispers.
I am staring into the garden.
I am watching the moon
wind its trail of golden slime around the oak,
over the stone basin of the fountain.
How can I tell her
I am thinking that transformations are not forever?

SUSAN MITCHELL

2

How much like the characters in fairy tales are the
people of the circus—the dwarfs and the fat lady, the sword
swallower and the tall man. Perhaps you've never run off and
joined a circus, or even considered it, but the chances are that,
as a child, you were fascinated by the circus performers and
what seemed to be a glittering life involving incredible skill and
daring. Daniel Halpern goes behind the scenes and imagines
what it would be like to be

THE LADY KNIFE-THROWER
for Sandy

In the gay, silver air of the tent
I'm at ease, fingers
at rest in my lap.
Before me the tools of my trade—
cleaned, well oiled and waiting
for the warmth of my hand, for the time
when the flick of my wrist will send them
out into the morning for their casual trip
to my husband's waiting body.
One at a time they plant themselves at his sides,
tucking in the air around his body.

At night, under the big top,
he is strapped to the board.
With a roll of drums I appear with my knives
and release my repertoire of throws.

There is no question in our lives of fidelity.
At night, after the knives are cleaned and placed
in their teakwood rack, we are all we desire.

Assuming the persona of the lady knife-thrower, Daniel Halpern brings us into the tent and we learn, first hand, how she feels about her knives, about her skill, and about her husband. We can surmise the drama of their lives together.

Write a poem in which you are a performer—the man on the flying trapeze, a tightrope walker, a lion tamer, a clown, an actress, a rock star. What kind of language would you use? What would you talk about? How do you feel about your work? Creating the image from the inside out, let us know what is under the make-up. Let us know the reality behind the act.

Sarah Burt, a student, writes sound and rhythm into the voice of a punk rock musician.

PUNK

My pink hair
Flames up
From my scalp
My boots click
My chains clink
Clatter
Black
I pose for a life
Night life
Black life
Short life
Alone
Known
And stolen
I live
Becoming someone else
Every day

In a poem that is very much like a story, Nancy Willard writes in the voice of Guiletta, the Birdwoman, who, as narrator, tells us what her life is like. As in a story, there are other characters seen through the eyes of the narrator—the clowns, the ringman, the dwarf, who is the villain, and the audience—all of these against the setting of the big top. Telling us about them, Guiletta tells us about herself.

THE FREAK SHOW

I am Giuletta, the bird woman. I married
the rain man and learned to fly.
Together we walked the high wire
over trees, churches, bridges, green fields,
straight into heaven. We saw the white seed
after a child blows it, and were much praised.
Though I had nothing but him, I craved no more.

Even in falling he blazed like a star.
The next night I went on, knowing I could not fall.
A brave girl, the clowns told me. Then I cried.
I knew that people who never fall forget
danger is all and their blood goes dumb.
Listen, the ring-man said to me one night,
You've lost your shape. You've got no grace.
You're old.

Waiting in the dark trucks I am content to watch,
to nibble the sweet fruits that the dwarf brings.
We walk among the orchards and hear
the silence of tensed feet on the blessed wire.
So much walking affects the appetite, Madam,
says the dwarf with a sucking leer.
And so much sorrow gives enormous hunger.

I am round and simple as a Persian plum,
so earth-shaped now no wire could hold me
or support the weight of my fallow grief.
When you hear the dwarf crying the measure
of my marvelous flesh, you will crowd in.
Blinded by footlights, I hear you wallow
and whisper in the pit below my chair.

My God! Arms like tree trunks cries a man's voice.
Must be hard on the heart, a woman blurts.
O friends, it is very hard on the heart.
For your delight I devour loaf after loaf
of stale bread, till the silken tents sink to rest
and wide-eyed children, bogeyed to bed,
remember my cavernous mouth with fear.

Sometimes I pick at my food like a child.
The taste of the wire in the apple hurts.

NANCY WILLARD

3

Other than through records and documents, one of the ways we find out about the lives of famous people is through their letters. Between the official dates of birth and death, their letters and the letters written to them provide the real information about what they were really like as people, what they thought and what they felt. But even the not so famous, even you, perhaps, save letters and cards because in their own tangible way they represent the sender. Ellery Akers' *Letters to Anna* is a narrative poem in the form of a series of letters, the first of which follows:

LETTERS TO ANNA, 1846–54

A Pioneer Woman's Journey

A fictional account of the life of a pioneer woman,
originally from Boston, who travels to a homestead
in Nebraska, and then through Wyoming, Utah, and
Nevada to California.

She finally settles in Volcano, a gold-mining town,
and becomes a school teacher.

Letter to Her Sister: Nebraska, 1846

Dear Anna,

Tonight there is a long slow cloud
moving outside the doorway like a dazed sheep,
and I miss you, miss watching the evenings with you,
falling so gently and variously.
It is all so much harder than we thought, Anna:
when we built this sod house
I never imagined the nights I would lie awake
touching the hard dry wall,
or the locusts pelting the field—horrible.
The goat is sick. When I go in the barn
it follows me with its patient eyes
and lies in the corner and heaves:
Joel is away so much; I don't know what to do.
Do you remember that old woman, Florence,
who used to sell eggs and snarl at us, with a face
as big as a pudding?

Oh, Anna, I am beginning to understand:
just lately, when I pass the schoolyard,
the children playing make me angry,
and I want to call after them, like a crazy,
"Fools, you don't know what's coming!"
I don't mean to worry you:
there are good times.
At night the stars stitch the hills together
with such clarity I am astonished;
I like picking the cabbages,
and in the morning, when the sun falls on the floor,
the cat licks my hand;
it wants salt, I suppose, but I take it as tenderness.
Do you remember our first house in Boston,
with the piano that loomed in the corner?
I used to wake up early
and pad on those thick carpets
to watch morning enter the dark windows.
There are no windows here.
Flour is dear, and the nights are getting cold and
    full of frost.
Thank you for the tablecloth.

Anna writes from the midst of the circumstances of her
life. The details of time present, the dry walls of the sod house
and the locusts pelting the field, are stitched together over the
background of time past, the piano and the thick carpets. Why
does Anna close her letter by mentioning the tablecloth? Although this is a letter, and is very much in the tone of a letter,
it is written in the lines of a poem. Each line turns to create the
suspense of the next line and to accumulate the drama of the
situation.

    Write a poem that is a letter or a journal entry. You
might write in the voice of

a mythological character	a bank teller
a historical figure	a file clerk
a surfer	an ambulance driver
an old person	a haircutter
an eminent scientist	a mountain climber

    who might be apologizing for something
    who is bragging

who, in retrospect, recognizes a fatal error
who has just fallen in love
who is writing a thank you note
who is making an excuse
who realizes his/her vulnerability

If it is a letter, make the scene come alive with specific places, dates or events. Where are you writing from? What is the news, the weather? Whom have you seen lately? Forget about "How are you? I am fine." Rather, begin in the middle.

Here in Athens the price of armor is sky high.
Soon it will be affordable
only by the gods.

If you are writing a journal entry, it should be so intimate that only you would read it. Make the person come alive with feeling, but avoid saying how you feel—sad, happy, discontent, envious. Let us discover how you feel by the things you tell us. In his journal, the Frog Prince writes,

In March I dreamed of mud, . . .
At night I cannot sleep.
I am listening to the dribble of mud . . .

Michael Goldfischer, a student, imagines Napoleon—

NAPOLEON

My generals were right.
It does snow that much.
It is that cold.
Women and cognac can't keep me warm.
The tides will turn tomorrow
maybe.
It's a long way home
but it might be shorter to Moscow
maybe.
It's too cold to take my hand
out of my coat
too cold to win a war
maybe
maybe.

4

The poet Stanley Kunitz writes,

I have walked through many lives
some of them my own . . .

In the same way, we are many people in our lives, sometimes,
several of them at the same time. The moody teenager to his
parents might be the model student to his teacher. The spoiled
brat to her sister is the loyal and generous friend. The boy who
forgets to mow the lawn and take out the garbage is the responsible baby-sitter for the next door neighbor. It depends upon
who's looking at whom and when. George Cuomo, in the voice
of a teacher, describes a former student.

ON THE DEATH OF A STUDENT HOPELESSLY FAILING MY COURSE

He died the day before the last exam,
Leaving parents a lifetime of saying
"He could have made it, poor boy." Poor boy, he
Could not. How little he could do in life!
He lacked whole galaxies of talents, lacked
Quickness of hand or foot or eye or mind,
Lacked will and ambition, lacked height and strength,
Lacked even hope, lacked means of being hurt.
He could swim well, he told me, and tried out,
And did not make the team, and did not mind.
Failure themed his small life, comforting him.
He died racing a fire-red sports car,
Soaring from the mountain roadway to spread
A giant arc across the still night sky.

We see the student through the eyes of the teacher and,
in one line, we have a momentary insight as to how his parents
saw him. "He could have made it, poor boy." Although both of
these views are different, both of them are sympathetic. Imagine
now that you knew the boy. You sat next to him in English or
you were there when he tried out for the swim team. How would
you have seen him? Write a poem in the voice of someone else
who knew him, the girl he called to go out on Saturday night, the
owner of the hardware store for whom he worked, the gas station

attendant who filled his tank. Imagine the personality of that person. What are the things that he or she would notice? What you say about the boy, the language you say it in, and the tone of your voice—sympathetic, indifferent, condescending, angry—will reveal not only the person you are talking about but who you are. We know the teacher by the way he reveals the boy. (What is he like?) Begin by deciding which role you will play. Imagine how you would feel. Then write your script. Specific examples of what he did or said, the way he sat in the classroom, how he walked away from the swim tryout, what he ate for lunch, will help to write him into life. Notice the specifics in the following excerpt from a student poem:

> . . . I would see him around school
> books sliding out
> from under his arms, pencils
> falling out of his pocket when he bent over,
> working the combination of his locker
> and overshooting the last number . . .
>
> LORI GILLIAR

5

Of all the people you might write about, the one you know the best is yourself. We know first hand our own masks and who we really are underneath the mask. We can surmise how others see us, but we know what we choose not to reveal. Write a poem in two parts. In the first stanza, keeping your distance, describe yourself as someone else might see you, a brother, a friend, a stranger, a parent. "He has always seen me . . ." "She continues to believe . . ." In the second stanza, describe yourself as you really are. Tell us something your brother, for instance, would have no way of knowing, a wish that you have, or a secret, or something you have done. "But he does not know . . ." or, "He will never know . . ." or, "One day I will tell him . . ." End the poem on this surprise revelation to the reader. None of what you write need be true—not the details, not the secret—but if you write in your own voice, someone real will emerge.

10
DREAMS AND
FANTASIES

1

The subject matter of dreams, the mystery of them, in fact the mastery of them has always been a fascination for people, and volumes have been written about how we dream and why we dream and what it all means. For all those who believe that dreams embody the images of the past, there are as many who swear they are a key to the future. What we can all agree on is that they explore a kind of no man's land or everyman's land. They take us through the looking glass and, in one way or another, we try to make head and tail of what we bring back. Whether we dream to order a portion of our lives, or whether we dream to make a dream come true, what we know is that we cannot choose our dreams and we cannot control them. For better or for worse, we are not responsible for them. Whether we dream in color or whether we dream in black and white, we accept that time and space are of no consequence. We accept the wildness of the dream image.

Which dreams are we most likely to remember? Probably nightmares and those dreams we dream just at the point of waking. But sometimes, somewhere in the day, we remember a dream when we see something or touch something that reminds us. What was that I dreamt last night? . . . and if we're lucky, the images begin to take shape. Sometimes we have the same dream again and again with the same or different props, like the falling dream or the flying dream or the dream of taking a test. This is the material Linda Pastan explores in

PASS/FAIL

"Examination dreams are reported to
persist even into old age . . ." *Time* Magazine

You will never graduate
from this dream
of blue books.
No matter how
you succeed awake,
asleep there is a test
waiting to be failed.
The dream beckons
with two dull pencils,
but you haven't even
taken the course;
when you reach for a book—
it closes its door
in your face; when
you conjugate a verb—
it is in the wrong
language.
Now the pillow becomes
a blank page. Turn it
to the cool side;
you will still smother
in all of the feathers
that have to be learned
by heart.

LINDA PASTAN

Rooted in reality, the items in the dream of blue books—the pencils, the book, the verb, the pillow—are raised to a super-real place. The feathers, for instance, must be learned by heart. Once we are caught up in the events of the dream, that it "beckons / with two dull pencils," we believe it. In the dream-world, it makes sense. Furthermore, we have been there.

Diane Wakowski, whose poem follows, begins with a series of surrealistic or dream images, the kinds of images that

might run amok through your mind almost at the point of
waking or moments before you settle into a dream sequence.

THE NIGHT A SAILOR CAME TO ME IN A DREAM

At the point of shining feathers
that moment when dawn
ran her finger along the knife edge sky;
at the point when chickens come out of the living room rug
to peck for corn and the grains like
old yellow eyes
roll as marbles across the floor;
at that sweet sprouting point when the seed of day
rests on your tongue,
and you haven't swallowed reality yet. Then,
then, yes, at that instant of shimmering new pine needles
came a dream, a blister from a new burn,
and you walked in,
old times,
no player piano or beer,
reality held my toes,
the silver ball of sleep was on my stomach,
the structure of a dream
like a harness
lowered over my head, around me,
and I cannot remember what you said, though the harbor
    was foggy,
and your pea coat seemed to drip with moisture.

Thirty years of travelling this ocean.

Perhaps you told me
you were not
dead.

DIANE WAKOWSKI

In which line do we know that this is not the first time
she's had this dream? What do you imagine might have been, "the
blister from the new burn," the particular, that triggered it? Maxine
Kumin's *The Longing to Be Saved*, which follows, is also a recurring
dream. "This happens whenever I travel." Which images move from
reality to surrealism?

THE LONGING TO BE SAVED

When the barn catches fire
I am wearing the wrong negligee.
It hangs on me like a gunny sack.
I get the horses out, but they
wrench free, wheel, dash back
and three or four trips are required.
Much whinnying and rearing as well.
This happens whenever I travel.

At the next stopover, the children take off
their doctor and lawyer disguises
and turn back into little lambs.
They cower at windows from which flames
shoot like the tattered red cloth
of dimestore devil suits. They refuse
to jump into my waiting arms, although
I drilled them in this technique, years ago.

Finally they come to their senses and leap
but each time, the hoop holds my mother.
Her skin is as dry and papery
as a late onion. I take her
into my bed, an enormous baby
I do not especially want to keep.
Three nights of such disquiet
in and out of dreams as thin as acetate

until, last of all, it's you
trapped in the blazing fortress.
I hold the rope as you slide from danger.
It's tricky in high winds and drifting snow.
Your body swaying in space
grows heavier, older, stranger

and me in the same gunny sack
and the slamming sounds as the gutted building burns.
Now the family's out, there's no holding back.
I go in to get my turn.

MAXINE KUMIN

Write a poem that is a dream. It may or may not be
based on a dream or dream image you've actually had. Try to
keep in mind that writing a poem, any poem, is very much like
having a waking dream in that you begin by accepting a signal

from your head—an image, a word, a phrase—and you allow yourself to go where it will take you. You permit it to unfold with as little guidance as you would give a dream. You owe nothing to sense and sequence, to size and place, only that in the end we should feel that the dream or the poem you have discovered might have been our own.

Here are some possibilities:

The Flying Dream	The Snow Dream
The Wind Dream	The Lateness Dream
The Food Dream	The Childhood Dream
The Running Dream	The Black Dream
The Hiding Dream	The Sea Dream

After you have finished writing your poem, or perhaps before, you might want to take a look at some of these poems by students.

THE WEDDING DREAM

White
Everything is white
Near, stifling white.
The *Wedding March* in a minor key
Plays, however.
People turn and stare
With cold eyes and white smiles.
My father takes my arm, leads me down the aisle
My father, the same stare, the same cold eyes, the same
    white smile
and the white haze begins to fade.
I'm not ready, I scream.
But it's time, they say tonelessly.
White roses are thrown, thousands
And I am stifled by the roses.
They push me
Down into the earth.

                                  SHARON LESSER

SWINGING

higher and higher
have to go higher
and reach
the snow in the sky
the rain's on my skin
and I have to go
higher
and reach the hand
with the ivory rings.

WENDY RISS

the race of my life

in my dream
there is a game
a race
the course of this race
my life
running
through blurry images
and past events
long forgotten
i relive
each day

looking back
i see my errors
and try to mend them
but
these can never be changed
this is only
a race
a game
a dream

ELLEN NOVEMBER

A DREAM

I sit down at my
desk to do my algebra homework.
Better do it quick or
it might melt.
Feeling a bit hungry
I eat my eraser. It's so

good I finish off the pencil
then the paper, the desk
the chair, the bookcase . . .
This happens every day. I've
gained 73 pounds, maybe 74
by now. I'm not sure because
I ate the scale.

FRANCESCA POMERANTZ

2

So much for the dreams of students. Taking it one step
further, what does the dog dream as he lies stretched in front of
the fire, his feet almost making the motion of running. Why the
small yelps? Is he hunting? Is he running away? Write a poem
that is the dream of an animal, a bird or a cat (or both), an
animal that is wild or one that is caged. Using the real world as
a springboard, make your jump. Or write the dream of an inanimate object such as a stone or a mirror, a broom or a shard of
glass. What would be its fear? What would be its dream come true?

3

Like dreams, there are fantasies that come to us unbidden
and without quite knowing how, we have moved from here to
there. Who has not built a castle in Spain? Places we've never gone,
parties we've never made, performances we've never given take on
their own structure. Imagined conversations, brilliant things we
wish we had said, or those we wish we had not, act out their scripts
as they will. But unlike dreams, we have a greater measure of control over some of our fantasies. We can, at will, lift ourselves from
the algebra book as we might imagine the *Girl on the Roof* does.

GIRL ON A ROOF

She'd gotten into the habit of going nights
to a secret ledge on the apartment house roof
on which she'd crawl until she was almost
over, out in the air above the city, the city

no longer itself,
its schoolyard blotted by the dark, but its bars,
drug stores, groceries, and luncheonettes
swirling with the melted ice creams
and spilled perfumes of colored lights,
the studded belts of avenues, the curves
of street lamps in the park the pearls
worn by a dusky sleeping princess, and the noise—comets
of horns and sirens, stray voices on corners thumped
into comic strips of rabbits fleeing wolves
with paws stuck luckily fast in pitch and howling, yowling,
yodeling at her (but harmless) from some radio or TV—oh,
the noise would weave a net to bounce against: no wonder
she'd lean from the edge and leap, yes, leap
straight into it, falling
through a bubble bath of air, her dress
blossoming around her while she hummed like the wind
with neon alphabets and traffic racing
from red to green past towers of ice cubes
where men and women sat frozen inside
like Mama and Daddy
who never saw her go by,
everything flew past
and she could just
look, look, look, and look

falling toward shimmer, except the shimmer firmed
and dirtied as she neared,
the news stand squatted
and was a hunk of news stand, a hunk, the sidewalk
kept sticking out its tongue,
and they were ready to call the ambulance now, they
    wanted her,
they needed her to finish this,
then she knew

she had to return—that, otherwise
the facts below would try to claim her
while only falling, doing nothing, made her happy,
so she'd let herself be pulled back to the roof
by force of will on the cables of her hair,
and she'd creep down the fire escape and sneak through
    a window
and find a Mama and Daddy as usual, saying,

"Where were you? Out?"
and she said, "Yes,
out," and locked herself in her room, as usual
and what she did there
no one knew,
she was so quiet and so neat.

JACK ANDERSON

Like a recurring nightmare, her fantasy had become a habit. It was a wish to be fulfilled, and like a dream, it moves in surrealistic imagery. The city is, "no longer itself." The street lamps are the pearls of a dusky princess. The noise will "weave a net to bounce against." It's only in the difference of control, the going and the coming back, that it's not a falling dream. Told very much like a story, the stanzas divide as the action changes and the plot develops. What is the effect of its being narrated in one long sentence?

In a lighter vein, but in its own way a wish come true, Jack Anderson invents the fantasy of a party train.

THE PARTY TRAIN

To bring joy and friendliness to the New York subway system, which is all too often bleak and indifferent, I propose that a special train be instituted to be known as The Party Train. Each day, this train would follow one or another of the city's existing routes, sometimes on the local, sometimes on the express tracks. No extra fare would be charged, the cars would be painted exactly the same as those of any other train, but inside there would be a perpetual party. The poles and straps would be festooned with streamers, and Japanese Lanterns would hang from the ceilings. Food and drink would be always available, ranging from corned beef to caviar, from beer to champagne. Strolling musicians would roam from car to car. And the last car would be transformed into a gigantic bed where anyone could take a date, no questions asked.

The Party Train would not only be fun to ride, the very knowledge of its existence would be a source of cheer. For the route it would follow on any given day would never be announced in advance, but would always come as a fresh surprise. Thus any citizen waiting in any

station could hope that the next train to pull in—
accompanied by a shower of confetti and a whiff of
pot smoke—would be The Party Train, so he could step
aboard and glut himself on cashew nuts and kisses from
the Battery to the Bronx. Or if he were in a local station
and The Party Train happened to be an express that day,
he would watch it rumble by, glimpsing paper hats and
saxophones bouncing in the front cars and naked bodies
flickering among the pillows at the back. Then he would
chuckle to himself, glad that there was something interesting to look at while waiting for the subway, and wish-
ing that tomorrow The Party Train might finally stop for
him.

JACK ANDERSON

Starting with the New York City subway system the way
it is, Jack Anderson bridges the gap from reality to fantasy by
the use of very specific details. We're on the track of the same
subway system, "following one or another of the city's existing
routes," but once inside the party train, once he's decided to
throw a party, detail upon detail, beginning with the streamers,
builds to a party to end all parties.

It's a prose poem* about hope, about an impossible wish
come true. Only a small leap of the imagination and you can
transform the school—every day a party in one or another of the
classrooms and you would never know when you came to French,
for instance, if that would be the place and the time, and the
teacher as maître d', would be serving pastry and pâté.

Write a poem that is a fantasy. It might be a real fantasy
in that it is truly yours and, like a tape, you replay it over and
over—a particular experience, perhaps, you as superhero. Some-
what different from a dream, the details of a fantasy might be
more realistic. There is corned beef and caviar. Although the
idea might be wild, there is not the distortion of time and space.
Change something, as Jack Anderson changes the subway system,
to something better, much better. Think along the lines of a
place, a procedure, a person, a conversation, a routine, a room.

*What makes a prose poem a poem? With the exception of the line break, the poet
draws upon all of the devices of poetry—metaphor and rhythm, rhyme and meter,
imagery and sound. If you read The Party Train aloud, you'll become more aware
of the sounds of corned beef to caviar, cashew nuts and kisses, Battery to the
Bronx, flickering among the pillows, hats and saxophones, and the like.

Latch on to an image and let it take you where it will. Ground us in the reality of specifics, "Starting on alternate Mondays . . ." "Next Wednesday it will be different . . ." "Once and only once . . ." "The table was set as usual . . ." But remember, "In the world of imagination," Richard Hugo says, "all things belong."

After you have written your poem, you might want to look at some of these poems by students. How does the form of each lend itself to the subject matter?

YO HO HO

The sun is blazing when I step into the sailboat with regret. I want to play baseball, not take a sailing lesson. To make matters worse, none of my friends is going. "Well," my sailing teacher says, "it's time to move out."

We move out of the shallows, and we are just leaving the boat basin when I realize I'm not in a Mercury K on the Great South Bay. I'm the captain of a present day pirate ship in the Caribbean. I am organizing a plunder party to take over the beautiful yacht, which we have just disabled with mortars and machine gun fire.

I have a patch over one eye and a wooden leg.

DOUGLAS SIMON

PRESENT

I present to myself
a jewel
glittering facets
of worldly fantasies
a separate pleasure
in each of its sides
so exact
yet so distorted
by images that enter
as one thing
and reflect another.

KATHY JACOBSON

STARTING OVER

For one hour a week
All eyes would close
In the middle of the day
And all thoughts made blank
And all feelings quiet
Then
In the middle of the day
Once a week
We could all
Start over.

DIANA SILVERMAN

PELICAN MAN

Most people think that I'm just a normal kid, but when I jump into a trash can, I reappear as Pelican Man and defend justice at all ends. I swoop down upon the bad guys, my craw taking in the wind, and I peck them with my beak. I proudly display the "P" on my chest. I'm the savior of justice and the defender of the Pelican Way. And in one mighty jump I leap into a trash can and transform into mild-mannered student—

JACOB COLLINS

NIGHT RAID

As I stood staring into the empty refrigerator I noticed a tiny man floating in the cream. I could barely hear him, yet I knew what he was saying. He drew me in closer. I could feel the door pushing against my back, and then it closed. He jumped from the eggs to the jelly, from the fruit to the peanut butter, where he slipped and was stuck. I grabbed for him. I am now as he is, so small, so energetic. I eat with all my heart's desire.

RICHARD DIMPERIO

4

One of the great escapes from the everyday world you live in is to invent another world, a far off place and a way of life that is entirely alien to your own, not unlike a looking-glass place, a Middle Earth, an Oz, or the lands that Gulliver visits. Consider how all of the things you take for granted would be different—things like the color of the sky, the nature of rain and snow (if there is any), of the sun or moon. Consider the differences in heat and light, weather and wind. Consider the concept of time, the world of animals and birds, the nature of trees and flowers. How do people pass the days? What are their tasks, their clothing, their food, their furniture, their diseases? Is there such a thing as the common cold? Do they marry? What are their views on education and on child rearing? What might be their motto or one of their proverbs?

Write a letter from that place to someone who has never been there. You might tell about one or about several of the things that go on, or you might describe one particular incident that will illustrate how different things are. Start in the middle with, "Yesterday . . ." "Today . . ." "Here . . ." "When you walk on the road . . ." "For days we have been listening for snakes . . ." "We keep an eye on the water . . ." Make clear how you feel about the fact, for example, that there is one hour of daylight every other day. You might write as a resident or a tourist. As a resident, you might ask for something particular to be sent. As a tourist, you may or may not end with, "Wish you were here." After you have finished writing your poem, or before, you will want to read the following poems by students.

OTHER WORLD LETTER

We keep an eye on the water,
here. We have to. Twice yesterday
it got up out of its bed, unannounced,
and left. Probably to visit the clouds; but we'll
never know for sure.

I met an inhabitant this morning.
Female, or so she said. Pretty, sorta.
Nice eyes. Especially the ones on her
head. The left one.

In answer to your question:
It's not that good. A lot of camp food
only more gamey. But it tends to grow
on you . . . literally.

I'm not the only Earthling over here,
you know. The other day I ran into Nancy.
Did she tell you? I took her to lunch.
The rest . . . is history.

Wish you were here,

Tim Radomisli

FROM ARAGON

Here there is magic,
real magic
not the fraudulent trickster type.
Wizards, warlocks, and witches
abound, and even a unicorn is not too rare.

The hillside is sprinkled
with sleep-inducing poppies.
The trees bend
with magenta pomagranates.
The sky is a swirl
a Van Gogh.

Behold—a dwarf
there, walking with an elf;
his coarse, hoary beard is
swarming around his face
his clodding boots are having difficulty
keeping in time with old elfie's
nimble green darters.

There in the distance now
almost blended into the blue haze above them
towers the mountain
at the peak of which abides
Lord Aragon
his castle, a wart
on the mountain's crown.

GILL METZGER

Some Notes on Self Editing

- What we are after here is honesty.

- We all have our own words, words that we've carried around with us for years, words that we've tried on and we're comfortable with. These are the words of "our voice" that tell the reader *someone* has written this poem. Be true to those words.

- Honesty also means the exact word rather than the well-that-will-do word. Poetry is concise—no time to fool around with approximations. "The best words," says Wallace Stevens, "in their best order."

- Part of the truth is saying what you have to say once and then moving on—each line a surprise to the one that precedes it.

- And part of the truth is having the courage to scratch your favorite image if the poem doesn't need it. It makes no difference whether you need it or not.

- The lines we need to get rolling may not necessarily be the lines the poem needs in the end. Like the armature of a sculpture, you can throw them away.

- A title cheats if it tries to account for what a poem can't do. A good title will make the reader go back. It will enrich the poem, not to mention the reader.

- Go in fear of adjectives. Get your mileage out of verbs.

- Open unexpectedly. Close unexpectedly.

- "Tell the truth," says Emily Dickinson, "but tell it slant."

Suggestions for
Using the Book in Class

This is a book to help students write poems. It may be used by students alone or in small groups, or by a teacher in a writing class or in any class in which poetry is taught. If it's used with a class, I believe it's important for the teacher to become a member of the class, a participant in the experience. It will take courage, as it does for the student, but there's something that takes place with the sharing of experience that will make everyone richer.

In setting up the actual classroom situation, I find that the best arrangement for the students, as well as for the teacher, is to be seated in a circle so that it's possible for every student to see every other student, which is probably the best arrangement for learning and sharing in any group situation. The atmosphere of the class should be easy so that the students will feel free to take risks, to say something or anything without fearing that others will laugh or be critical. The atmosphere should be such that it will permit the student to discover something he or she already has—a knowledge of how to use language, a unique way of looking at the world.

In each chapter, the suggestions for writing move from a very clear, direct set of possibilities for developing a poem to a more open expression. With the exception of the first chapter, which is a way to ease in, chapters may be used in any order. Choose the exercise that *you* would like to try, the poems that *you* would like to read. One exercise, including discussion, writing, and reading, will take approximately an hour, but each could easily take longer. Each of the model poems has been selected because it can be directly related to the experiences of the students. The poems at the end of the chapter and throughout each chapter are variations of the particular poetry idea to be developed. Most of them are by contemporary poets. Most of them have not appeared in anthologies before.

Beginning each lesson with a class discussion will loosen things up. Questions to initiate the discussion are part of the material contained in each chapter. For example, in the chapter, *Then*, in a discussion of the imaginary games played as a child, the teacher might begin by describing a game that he or she played and then elicit similar experiences from the students. When I have done the exercise on school poems, I have begun the class by serving graham crackers and warm apple juice in small paper cups. Reminding them through an immediate sense experience made those early classrooms very real to the students. Especially at the beginning of the unit, authentic writing requires a high degree of readiness. While the ideas are still flying, read the model poem aloud. Clarify whatever might need clarifying. Then you might read the examples of the poems other students have written. Writing is best done then, in the classroom, while the class is warmed up.

The initial writing time should be about fifteen minutes. The students should be encouraged to write quickly without censoring. The teacher should write, too. This is not the time to worry about first lines or spelling or punctuation. Let the ideas and images flow—one idea or image reaching back to another. There will be time later to make selections. After everyone has finished, there should be enough time for each person to read his or her poem aloud. The class should close on a sense of sharing and a sense of completion.

After the first meeting, I have found it an effective teaching tool to have copies of some of the poems from the previous lesson (everyone's eventually) on worksheets. These might be typed on ditto sheets by the students and used as a bridge between meetings and as an opportunity to read what might otherwise have been missed in the oral reading the previous lesson. I ask students to comment on those words, those phrases, those lines that really work for them. I try to elicit why—is it the sound, is it the particular image evoked, the choice of a special verb, a surprising comparison, etc.? This is the time to work with language, to use, if you wish, the technical terms of poetry. The positive things, the things that work for them, will be tried again by the student who wrote them and by those who read them and heard them. They will learn by what is good. Toward the end of the experience, you may want to be more specific about self-editing.

In the end, the idea is to establish an ease with poetry, the kind of knowledge and appreciation that can only come from having written it, the understanding that a poem is not an object to be decoded and divided according to nomenclature, rather a tool, a way of helping the student find his own poem. Although students may not continue to write, "the exhilaration," says Galway Kinnell, "of speaking, as if magically, from the center of one's being, is itself a blessing, and worth doing, even if only in one's adolescence."

Title Index

Author Index

*Additional poems by these poets can be found in books and periodicals.